LUSH

LUSH

A SEASON *by* SEASON

CELEBRATION OF

Craft Beer

AND

Produce

JACQUELYN DODD

S
SURREY BOOKS

AN AGATE IMPRINT

CHICAGO

First edition published October 2019

Printed in China

Library of Congress Cataloging-in-Publication Data

Names: Dodd, Jacquelyn, author.
Title: Lush : a season-by-season celebration of craft beer and produce / by Jacquelyn Dodd.
Description: First edition. | Chicago : Surrey, an Agate Imprint, 2019. | Includes index. |
Identifiers: LCCN 2019003159 (print) | LCCN 2019004419 (ebook) | ISBN 9781572848337 (ebook) | ISBN 1572848332 (ebook) | ISBN 9781572842762 (cloth) | ISBN 1572842768 (cloth)
Subjects: LCSH: Cooking (Beer) | LCGFT: Cookbooks.
Classification: LCC TX726.3 (ebook) | LCC TX726.3 .D64 2019 (print) | DDC 641.6/23--dc23
LC record available at https://lccn.loc.gov/2019003159

10 9 8 7 6 5 4 3 2 1   19 20 21 22 23

Art direction and cover design by Morgan Krehbiel
Cover photo by Jacquelyn Dodd

Surrey Books is an imprint of Agate Publishing. Agate books are available in bulk at discount prices. For more information, visit agatepublishing.com.

For Nick:
For being my person,
for our two-man parties,
and for a love so good I
hardly deserve it.

CONTENTS

LUSH

/ ˈləsh /

ADJECTIVE: growing vigorously, characterized by abundant produce

SLANG: intoxicating liquor

INTRODUCTION

THE BREEZE GENTLY CUTS ACROSS THE PATIO DECK, loosening the grip the summer sun has wound around the afternoon. My hand is on the base of a beer glass, its contents warming quicker than I can consume it, the flavors changing with every sip and every degree it warms. A plate of ripe watermelon sprinkled with feta and pickled red onions sits in front of me, and I realize how well it all goes together. Not just the sweetness of the watermelon against the briny onions, or even the way the carbonation of the slightly malty summer ale cuts it in the perfect way, leaving me wanting more of everything. It's how it *all* goes together. The sun, the afternoon, the heat, the food, the drink—it all mixes together to form a combination that goes far beyond flavors.

Experiences that surround any meal leave an indelible mark on our perception of the enjoyment, and there is no greater backdrop to our experiences than the seasons they take place in. The way the air smells in the spring, the crunching of leaves under our feet in the fall, the sting of frost-spiked breath in our lungs on a winter morning, the heat of the summer sun against bare arms. And there isn't a more tangible punctuation to each season than the food that comes out of the ground when the weather is just right. Sure, you *can* have a tomato grown out of season, but it's a far cry from the real thing: picked in the heat, ripe, red, and heavy with flavor.

The ingredients for beer mostly come out of the ground, too. Some ingredients are seasonless—barley is malted and then dried, hops are dried and packaged as either cones or pellets, and yeast is not subject to the same rules that other living things are. But these aren't the ingredients I'm referring to. I'm talking about the ingredients that flavor a pumpkin beer or a blood orange gose—or maybe a lemon hefeweizen or a ginger saison. To make those beers, a thoughtful brewer needs more than barley, hops, and yeast.

Most of the time, meticulous craft brewers use ingredients that are in season, grown within driving distance of the mash tuns and fermenters they'll soon take up residence in. These brewers are also thinking about where the beer they're about to make is going to be consumed—on a patio in the sun or near a fireplace in a winter cabin. Beer is part of a larger experience, and brewers innately feel this as they brew beer for each season, taking into account what drinkers will be doing and where they're likely to be when they imbibe.

Say you are hiking in the woods on a late summer afternoon, the dust clinging to your sweaty legs, your t-shirt thin over your sunbaked shoulders. You won't be reaching into that cooler for an imperial peanut butter stout. Or on a chilly winter evening, in that forgotten week between Christmas and New Year's, sitting in your oversize wool sweater warming your fingers by the cabin fire, you'll be less likely to crave a lemon ISA and more likely to pour an imperial caramel stout.

This book celebrates the fact that beer is as seasonal as produce. Recipes change as the seasons bring different weather, ingredients, and experiences the last season didn't offer. This book is for those who allow their lives, plates, and pints to shift with the seasons and want to observe and use what the earth has to give us when it's ripe and ready to be picked.

Seasonal beer is one of the fastest-growing categories of craft beer in the United States. Love it or hate it, pumpkin beer may be the reason this trend began its fervid growth spurt, but as of now, those quintessential squash-infused beers are being outpaced by other, more exciting seasonal offerings. Each season, we see new beers made with in-season

Hops and malt
are essential
ingredients in
making beer,
providing the
bitterness and
the sweetness
to create a
balanced flavor.

produce, brewed to be enjoyed most fully during that time of year. Peach beers, for instance, are growing in popularity as these fuzzy little fruits find their way into every type of beer, from sours to barrel-aged Belgians. Summer is full of citrus and berries, which turn up in everything from shandies, which are equal parts beer and fruit juice, to hefeweizens, bright and easy-drinking wheat beers.

Fall is one of the most exciting times of year for the craft beer fan, and for reasons that have nothing to do with squash. In the late summer, hops come into season, harvested just this one time a year. For only about twelve hours after hops are picked from the bine, brewers are able to use the soft, fresh, bright buds—full of natural lupulin oils—to brew beer. Lupulin oils bring a brightness, a freshness that's either dulled or completely lost once the hops are dried. With notes of tropical fruit, grass, and even coconut, fresh-from-the-bine hops are an incredible gift to any fall brewing schedule. This rare and brilliant opportunity brings us what's called "fresh hop" or "wet hop" beer. The rest of the year, brewers use hops that have been dried right after harvest. Dry hops have far less lupulin and a very different flavor profile, and most of the beer you drink throughout the year is made with them. However, fresh hop beers will be gone before the season is over, creating a fevered rush to any taproom pouring this liquid gold.

Winter beers are made to match the season. They tend to be darker in color and warmer in flavor than warm-weather beer. They are also frequently spiced to match the food we're serving, and often higher in alcohol by volume (ABV). Winter is when we are finally able to sample barrel-aged beers that were brewed months (even years) ago and left to age in secondhand liquor barrels. Winter beers are made specifically for the chilly weather and the deep-flavored foods of the season, working perfectly with the experiences of those colder months.

I want to be clear about one thing, though: this book isn't about pairing a pint of beer with a plate of food. It's about using beer as an important ingredient in the dish—a union that is far more intrinsic and elemental than a simple pairing. Beer brings with it flavors, grains, leavening agents, and even preservative properties that no other baking liquid can match. Each

WHAT IS DRY HOPPED BEER?

When you hear "fresh hop beer" and "wet hop beer," you may think of "dry hopped beer." Somewhat confusingly, beer made with dried hops is not necessarily dry hopped beer. Rather, this term refers to a step in the brewing process when brewers add hops after the boil. Think of adding a bag of tea to hot water: the hops steep in the hot water rather than cook in the boil.

For decades, cooking with beer was looked down on as a frat boy endeavor. People didn't understand the power of craft beer as an ingredient and how arguably superior it is to wine when it comes to cooking.

recipe in this book is made with beer: beer that is part of the season it's cooked in, beer that should be enjoyed in the season it's intended for—just like the produce in your garden or at your local farmers market.

For decades, cooking with beer was looked down on as a frat boy endeavor (or a low-class alternative to the French propensity for including wine in recipes), and the kind of food most commonly associated with beer—heavy, fatty, meaty, fried, or grilled pub and cookout fare—was neither complex nor refined. In 2012, when I started my website, TheBeeroness.com, this was the attitude and confusion I commonly faced. No, I wasn't making "silly" recipes or novelty food—I was making beautiful, complex dishes that echoed the beautiful flavors of the craft beers that I had fallen in love with. At the time, people didn't understand the power of craft beer as an ingredient and how arguably superior it is to wine when it comes to cooking.

Luckily, this narrow mind-set has shifted dramatically over the past few years. Brewpubs have been steadily upping their menu game, craft breweries often have killer kitchens to match their inventive brews, and even high-end restaurants these days frequently include beer pairings right alongside wine pairings. For those in the know, cooking with beer is no longer reserved solely for camping trips or your weird uncle's chili. It's a culinary adventure, one that fits right into the idea of farm-to-table eating, and a way to explore the fantastic flavors that craft brewers spend so much time developing.

This book is both evidence of this shift, and counterprogramming. Most beer and beer-as-ingredient cookbooks on the market still play into an outdated view of beer and food, one that emphasizes beer as a novelty ingredient or focuses only on recipes you'd find at your local dive bar. Cooking with beer, and beer in general, is no longer a poor man's endeavor—or just a man's, for the matter. The beer world is full of diversity, important flavors, interesting people, and constant inno-vation. It's an exciting time to be in beer, and it's fascinating to watch it continue to grow and evolve. It's time our home kitchens caught up with what is happening in the world of craft beer.

THIS BOOK'S TERROIR

I live and write from a little corner of the United States of America called the Pacific Northwest. Its varied landscapes offer up an impres-sive number of native plants each season, and it is home to the lion's share of hops grown in this country. I mention this because you may live in a different part of the world, with different seasons and different growing patterns. Keep that in mind when you're thumbing through this book, and be aware that, where you live, the food may pop out of the ground on a different calendar. Use the appropri-ate recipes whenever your fruits and vegetables come into season, enjoy them with local beer, and don't be too bothered if your "spring" isn't the same as mine.

> Use what is in season for you, and don't be too bothered if your "spring" isn't the same as mine.

THE CASE FOR FROZEN

It's an "F" word in certain circles, a word that can conjure up images of lazy cooks and ice crystallized on inferior foods. Let that go. Let fall away the idea that frozen is always bad and fresh is always good. I was in the sorting facility of a small, family-run strawberry farm in Oxnard, California, when that all became clear to me.

"This is one we'll freeze," the owner of the farm told me, gently lifting the ripest, reddest, juiciest strawberry from a pallet of berries with his large, paw-like hand. Weathered and cracked, but clean and gentle, his fingers framed the little gem for display. "It's perfect, but it's so ripe that it'll get destroyed during shipping. It'll be squished, or it'll rot before it can be enjoyed. And that would be a shame—look how perfect it is." He looked at it the way some would look at a newborn kitten; he wanted to protect it.

Produce that is frozen in season is often the best and ripest, making it far, far superior to anything grown out of season in a greenhouse. If I call for an ingredient that you can't get fresh where you live, look for it frozen as an excellent alternative. Of course, once the kitten-like strawberry is frozen, it can't be brought back to life like a villain in a sci-fi movie. It can, however, be cooked and enjoyed after it's thawed (and this sentence officially makes me regret my decision to use a kitten analogy). Freezing, like canning, can be an excellent way to preserve the food from your garden when it's in abundance.

> Freezing, like canning, can be an excellent way to preserve the food from your garden when it's in abundance.

INGREDIENTS: WHAT I USED, WHAT I DIDN'T, AND WHY

A book that celebrates the beauty of seasonal produce shouldn't include meat; it's an unnecessary distraction. Produce is part of the earth, shifting and responding to the seasons with new and abundant offerings, refusing to grow without extreme measures outside its natural growing patterns. While there are specific times of year when certain types of seafood or meat are more abundant and available, they aren't as heavily dependent on season and weather. Pigs, cows, and chickens all exist in nature during all parts of the year; naturally grown fruits and vegetables don't. For produce to truly be the star of the show in this book, I decided to leave meat out and focus on making plants the center of each dish.

I am not a vegetarian, at least not anymore. I spent three years navigating the world of meat-free living—bringing marinated portobello mushrooms to cookouts to substitute for burger patties, eating mostly side dishes when invited to dinner parties, being eye-rolled by strangers when I asked for the vegetarian meal on an international flight.

Although I eat meat now, I'm thoughtful about it, eating it rarely and only when I know it's high quality and responsibly raised. I opt for vegetarian meals more often than not. For various reasons, more and more people are opening themselves up to the idea that meat-free meals aren't exclusive to vegetarians. For some, it's an ethical issue born from worries of animal welfare. Others are concerned about the negative impact meat production has on the environment, and still others limit their meat intake for health reasons.

This book is for everyone. I don't want it to be seen as something exclusive to those who abstain from meat altogether. Good food is good food—and that's what I want to offer the world.

It should be noted that I don't use any fake meat, or anything that seems to be a meat substitute. I rarely used them when I was a vegetarian, as substitutes can make recipes feel "without" in a way that I don't like. I didn't want a blatant reminder that meat isn't included—I want the recipes to be shining examples of how fantastic food can be when you have the entire spectrum of plants to play with.

Each season offers far more in the way of fresh fruits and vegetables than I am able to provide recipes for in this book. For each season, I chose ten different fruits, vegetables, or herbs to focus on, giving you two recipes for each.

It wasn't always an easy choice, but I put a lot of thought into the

This book is for everyone. I don't want it to be seen as something exclusive to those who abstain from meat altogether. Good food is good food—and that's what I want to offer the world.

ingredients I chose for each season. Although my own favorites weighed heavily, I tried to focus on what is available in abundance throughout the country and the world, ingredients that wouldn't be too difficult to source no matter where you live. I also considered what is universally popular and well liked, favoring what I'd imagine you'd most want recipes for. In some cases, the produce I chose is in season for multiple seasons or even year-round. In those cases, I placed them in the season when they come into peak abundance. When an ingredient is harvested through multiple seasons (most are), I use that ingredient across all the seasons that it's harvested. On occasion, I use an ingredient in a shoulder season in frozen form—good thing you froze that produce when it was available!

At the beginning of each recipe section, I go into more detail about what I chose and why. I'm thrilled to share these recipes with you and satisfied with the choices I made for each season. I hope you are, too.

IS THAT A PIG IN YOUR PINT GLASS?

The basic ingredients for beer are water, hops, malt, and yeast, all of which are clearly vegan. But, that's before the brewers get their hands on them. From creative ingredients to elaborate purifying measures, plenty of beer goes from vegan beginnings to not-even-vegetarian beverages once they reach the taproom.

Sometimes, the de-veganized beer is easy to spot: a milk stout that uses lactose or a honey kölsch, for example. But more often than not, we are in the dark as to whether an animal part has made its way into our pint glass. Since the CDC, the TTB, and the FDA (and all the other acronym-loving agencies that regulate what we consume) do not require breweries to disclose the use of animal byproducts in the processing of their food or beverages, animal parts almost always get left off the label. Although no one is purposefully trying to deceive, you might have to do some sleuthing to figure out if there's an animal byproduct in your beer.

The biggest culprits are what brewers use to clarify beer. While clarifying is often done with non-animal ingredients (or a centrifuge machine), it's still common for breweries to use items like gelatin or fish bladders as clarifying agents, rendering beer not only non-vegan, but also non-vegetarian. There is also the issue of foam control. I'm not talking about the frothing of the mouth that occurs when your favorite stout is on nitro, but rather the desire brewers have to give you that perfect amount of foam head on your pints. To gain control of this, brewers have been known to use pepsin (made from pigs) or albumin (made from animal blood or egg whites) to give you the perfect pour.

But if you are one of the growing numbers of craft beer–loving veggie devotees, don't despair. Countless breweries are hip to your vibe, and vegan beer is a concern for many. When it comes to finding out if your beer was made sans beasts, Google is your friend. Websites such as Barnivore.com provide a great and growing list of vegan-friendly breweries and beers. And don't be afraid to ask the brewers; they'll know if you are safe to enjoy the pints they pour, and they are always up for a friendly chat about their brewing processes. Once you have yourself an arsenal of animal-free breweries and beers you adore, it'll be smooth sailing for your safe beer consumption.

KITCHEN TIPS

WEIGHT > VOLUME. Weigh your ingredients! For those still using the ol' cups and tablespoons route, an inexpensive kitchen scale can vastly improve your cooking. This is why I provide weight measurements in grams in addition to the US standard units you are likely used to. Why? It's far, far more consistent and reliable than measuring by volume. Flour is the most obvious example. Depending on how long your flour was stored, how much moisture is in the air, and whether you scooped or spooned your flour into the measuring cup, you could be using *twice* as much as you intended. Have you ever made a cake recipe that turned out awesome one day and too dry the next, even though you followed the recipe exactly both times? It could be that you inadvertently used far more flour than intended. Measuring by weight—yes, even liquids!—takes the guesswork out of cooking: 120 grams will always be 120 grams, no matter how you store it, scoop it, or pack it. Plus, you don't have to dirty as many dishes.

TEMPERATURE IS IMPORTANT. If it wasn't, I wouldn't mention it. Did the recipe call for softened (room-temperature) butter but you used cold? It will not react the same, and your result will be compromised and possibly ruined.

OUNCES AREN'T ALWAYS OUNCES. This drives me to drink. I'm not sure exactly who decided to call them both "ounces," but weight ounces and fluid ounces aren't the same thing. Weight ounces are supposed to be used to measure solids, and fluid ounces are supposed to be used to measure liquids. But this often isn't specified in cookbooks or on measuring devices, and people sometimes get confused. For instance, if you accidentally used your *fluid* measuring cup to measure chocolate chips to the 8-ounce line, it would *weigh* only 6 ounces. If a recipe calls for 4 ounces of grated cheese, you could end up with ½ cup if you measured with a fluid measuring cup but only ¼ cup if you used weight ounces. Most of the time (as in this book) when ounces are called for, it refers to weight and not volume. Meaning, if I ask for 8 ounces of chocolate, don't break out your liquid measuring cup. Use a scale (or read the package; it will be listed on there). Lucky for us, water (and beer) are even: 8 ounces by volume is also 8 ounces by weight.

SALT. This may be one of the most important factors in truly great food and something that home cooks tend to be light-handed on. Salt your food at every step when you can, and taste as you go. If your final dish tastes just a little "dull," try adding a bit of salt; its main purpose is to enhance flavor, and it truly makes everything taste better.

STANDARD PANTRY INGREDIENTS

Throughout this book, I tend to use some of the same ingredients over and over, pantry staples I rely on heavily as I develop and test recipes. For instance, I always use **kosher salt** or **sea salt**, never iodized table salt. I find that table salt, with its over-abundance of iodine, lends an unappealing bleachy taste to food that I don't care for. The salt crystals in kosher salt are bigger and less compact, making it less likely that you'll oversalt your food. Keep in mind while you're making these recipes that using table salt instead of kosher salt (as called for) is likely to make the resulting dish overly salty.

I also always, always, always use **unsalted butter**. Why, you might ask, do I call for unsalt-ed butter and also salt in a recipe? Good question, and the answer is simple: I want to control the amount of salt in

a recipe. There is no standard amount of salt in a stick of salted butter, leaving me to wonder how much salt I actu-ally added when using salted butter. Was it ¼ teaspoon? Or maybe 2 teaspoons? The only way to know is if I add it my-self, separate from the butter.

I also always use **good-quality extra virgin olive oil**, even when the price skyrockets and I sit in the grocery aisle de-bating how much I really want to pay for it. Good olive oil really does make a difference. You don't have to buy the top-shelf variety, but try to steer clear of the cheapest one out there. If you do splurge on the fancy stuff, save it for when you're making a vinaigrette. Unlike other applications, like pan-frying, the flavors of the oil will be present in your salad and make a great difference.

If there is one ingredient I implore you to spend as much money as you can on, it's **free-range eggs**. In this case, the difference between cheap and expensive is staggering. Cheap eggs come from factory farms that cut corners and sacrifice quality for a bottom line. The farms that mistreat animals and their own workers are able to charge less, while the farms that are responsible and thoughtful must charge more because being equitable and ethical costs more. Not only that, but the eggs from free-range chickens have *far* better flavor. Just look at the yolks. Cheap yolks are light yellow and anemic looking, while good-quality eggs are dark golden and full of flavor. Try, if you can, to find a local chicken farmer to source eggs from; they tend to be the best you'll ever eat, and you'll be supporting a local farm. It's a double win.

KEEP THESE ON HAND

WHAT YOU'LL NEED TO MAKE THESE RECIPES (JUST ADD SEASONAL BEER AND PRODUCE)

ESSENTIALS

FATS

coconut oil

extra virgin olive oil

full-fat canned coconut milk

neutral oil, such as canola, vegetable, or grapeseed

toasted sesame oil

unsalted butter

vegetable shortening

ACIDS

apple cider vinegar

balsamic vinegar

red wine vinegar

sherry vinegar

white vinegar

white wine vinegar

whole lemons

whole limes

SEASONINGS

cayenne pepper

chili powder

Creole seasoning

curry powder

dried oregano

dried thyme

garam masala

garlic powder

ground allspice

ground cinnamon

ground cumin

ground ginger

ground and whole nutmeg (grate your own with a Microplane for the best flavor!)

kosher salt

mustard powder

onion powder

paprika (sweet and smoked)

pure vanilla extract

red pepper flakes

reduced-sodium soy sauce

whole black peppercorns

SWEETENERS

golden (light) brown sugar

granulated sugar

high-quality local honey

powdered sugar

pure maple syrup

STAPLES

FRIDGE

buttermilk

burrata

cotija

cream cheese

Dijon mustard

feta

fresh mozzarella

goat cheese

gouda

Gruyère

half-and-half

heavy cream

large free-range eggs

mascarpone

Mexican crema

Parmigiano-Reggiano (the real stuff)

plain whole-milk yogurt

puff pastry

ricotta

sour cream

tahini

whole milk

PANTRY

baking powder

baking soda

canned beans (chickpeas, great Northern, black, etc.)

canned hominy

corn tortillas

cornmeal

cornstarch

dried pasta (manicotti, strozzapreti, lasagna, etc.)

fast-rising instant yeast

flour (all-purpose and bread)

fresh bread (baguette, brioche, slider buns, etc.)

nuts (almonds, hazelnuts, pecans, etc.)

peanut butter

pearled farro

reduced-sodium vegetable broth

rice (Arborio and long-grain white)

rice noodles

rice paper sheets

tomato paste

unsweetened cocoa powder

PRODUCE

chilies (serrano, jalapeño, and poblano)

fresh ginger

fresh herbs (parsley, basil, thyme, oregano, rosemary, mint, etc.)

garlic

onions (green, sweet, white, and red)

shallots

FAVORITE FLAVORS

chopped chipotle in adobo

espresso powder

gochujang (spicy-sweet Korean chili paste)

hot pepper sauce

mirin (Japanese rice cooking wine)

red curry paste

sambal oelek (Indonesian chili paste)

Sriracha

tamarind paste

BEER AS AN INGREDIENT

SO, WHY WOULD YOU COOK WITH BEER? Why not just drink it like a normal person? Great question—I'm glad you asked! Cooking with alcohol isn't new. From the wine in coq au vin to the sweet liqueur in cherries jubilee, cooking with booze is a time-honored tradition. But why beer instead of wine, rum, or liqueur? Let's dive in.

Unlike most varieties of alcoholic beverages that contain only one or two ingredients, beer offers you at least four. Each ingredient lends something different to your dish, qualities you'd be hard-pressed to find with any other liquid. The hops act as a mild preservative as well as a unique and powerful flavor, the combination of the yeast and carbonation serves as a mild leavening agent that lends an extra puff to your baked goods, and the malted barley is a beautiful flavor that complements everything from pizza dough to chocolate cake. These ingredients come together to make a super liquid that's perfect for baking and cooking.

The flavor of beer shouldn't be overlooked as a main factor in pouring a pint into your pot. It can deglaze your pan as well as add a nice malty note to your chili. But if you find that the beer flavor is too present, use a beer that is less hoppy next time. The hop flavors can be overwhelming in a highly hopped beer like an IPA, so switch to a pilsner or a kölsch for something more mild. Or, in a savory dish, replace half of the beer with something else, like broth or water. If, on the other hand, the beer flavor wasn't as present as you'd like, try the opposite. Replace an English brown ale with an American brown ale, as they tend to be far hoppier. Or use a double IPA (DIPA) instead of a pale ale. You get the idea.

Each recipe in this book includes a recommendation for which type of beer to use—not specific brands, but a category and description. I encourage you to explore your local beer scene, asking taproom jockeys and brewers to help you find the best fit for each category asked for.

MALT VERSUS HOPS

Possibly the most important factor to consider when deciding which beer to use in any given recipe is whether the flavor is more malty (sweet) or hoppy (bitter). When choosing a beer for each recipe, try to stick to the style recommended. When you can't, try to choose a beer that's similar on the malt-to-hop scale. For instance, if a recipe calls for a stout, don't use an IPA, as the overall flavor may be far too bitter. However, a porter or even a brown ale would make a good stand-in because the malt profiles are similar. Or, if a recipe calls for a pilsner and you can find only a pale lager, that will do just fine, since both have relatively low hop and malt profiles. If you're unsure about how to choose a beer that has a similar hop or malt profile, ask the person at your local bottle shop to help.

Malt and hops are the yin and yang of beer. Malt provides the sweetness and sugar yeast needs for fermentation, while hops provide bitterness and flavor.

BASIC STYLES OF BEER

I provide a rundown of seasonal beers at the start of each chapter, but here's some general information about beer and how it's made. First, the idea of ales versus lagers is something you've always wondered about, isn't it? The distinction between the two is simple, but the beers in each category are starting to blur more and more each day.

The main difference between ales and lagers is the type of yeast used. Ales are fermented at a higher temperature and use a yeast that likes to kick it at that temperature. Thus, the fermentation time is much quicker; the higher temperature speeds things up. Lagers were first created in Europe less than 300 years ago. Compare this to ales, with a history that predates written language, and lagers are mere infants. Lagers, as you may have already guessed, are fermented at much colder temperatures using yeast strains that like it chilly. Lager yeast doesn't always work at ale temperatures, and vice versa.

For decades the distinctions were clear: IPAs, stouts, and hefeweizens were all ales, while bocks, pilsners, and märzens were all lagers. These days, brewers like to get a little creative and will lager an IPA (known in that case as an IPL) or a stout or any other beer formerly known as "ale" that they can get their hands on—all in the name of experimentation. The same goes for lagers being aled. So, instead of trying to break it all down with ales versus lagers, let's just talk categories in general terms, regardless of the yeast and fermentation times used.

PALE ALE

A **pale ale** is so named because it is relatively lighter than its darker ale counterparts, such as porters and stouts. This style has its origins in England. **India pale ale (IPA)** is a slightly more bitter version. They were originally produced for British soldiers stationed in India, but they are now a staple of craft breweries. **Session IPAs** (also called **India session ales** or **ISAs**) are newer to the scene; they are lower in ABV than regular IPAs.

BROWN ALE

Brown ales are vastly underappreciated brews in the craft beer world. Like peacoats, they've never really been the hottest ticket, but nor will they ever really go out of style. The original brown ales were brewed in England and named after the brown malt used in their brewing process. At one time, they were nearly extinct as a style, but the humble brown ale was saved by home brewers decades ago. Maybe it was because brown ales are reliable and tasty, or maybe it's just an easier style to brew than a stout. Either way, I'm grateful.

STOUT

Don't let these beasts fool you—they're gentle giants. They look fierce with their inky good looks, but they have a much milder, sweeter flavor than you might expect. **Stouts** were born from another dark beer, the **porter**. Porters and stouts are both made with grains that have been roasted to near blackness, giving them their inky color and toasted flavors. Porters came first, gaining wide popularity across Europe in the eighteenth century. Once brewers started to tinker with the formula (as they often do) and the ABV was raised, the term **stout porter** was born, referring to a stronger version of a porter. Today, the ABV of a dark beer has no bearing on whether it will earn a stout or porter designation. For example, Guinness, the world's most popular stout, has an ABV of only 4.2 percent, and very few porters are at or below that level. **Oatmeal stouts** are a popular version, brewed with oats for a smooth mouthfeel and slightly less bitter taste. **Milk stouts** are beers brewed with lactose sugars from milk; because it's a type of sugar that can't be used by yeast in fermentation, it lends a creamy sweetness to the stout.

WHEAT BEER

As you can guess, a wheat beer is a beer made with wheat. **Hefeweizen** (which literally means "yeast wheat" in German) is the most common. Wheat beers were first brewed in Bavaria in the sixteenth century and made their way to the United States with German immigrants in the

---

WHAT IS AN IMPERIAL BEER?

"Imperial" added to the name of any style of beer means that the beer is higher in alcohol content than a standard beer of the same style. For instance, an imperial IPA has a higher ABV than a standard IPA.

nineteenth century. It's true that any beer *can* be made with wheat—if you look hard enough, you'll find a wheat IPA, a wheat stout, a wheat sour (brewers, amiright?!)—but traditionally, the category has been dominated by hefeweizens and **witbiers** (also known as **white ales**), wheat beers with origins in Belgium and the Netherlands. You may also see **weissbier**, a German ale that's made with a high ratio of wheat in the grain bill. Wheat beers are generally smooth, approachable, and low on hop bitterness.

BELGIAN ALE

Buckle up, I'm about to shock you: **Belgian ales** originated in Belgium. (I know, I know, you'd never have guessed!) The history of Belgian ales is fascinating, though. The majority of the most iconic and sought-after Belgian beers in the world are, and have always been, brewed by monks in monasteries in Belgium. The many different types of Belgian beers vary when it comes to ABV, color, and carbonation level, but they also have a lot in common. Belgian ales are well known for being highly malty, sweet, fruity, and low on hops. Types of Belgians include **Trappist** (named after the monks who brew it), **abbey** (not necessarily brewed in one, though), **dubbel** (uses caramelized sugar), **tripel**, and **quadrupel** (a.k.a. **quad** or **Belgian strong dark ale**). It should be noted that a tripel isn't "one more than" a Belgian dubbel (as you might assume), because beer is weird like that. It just means that you have three times the malt as a typical abbey (although it isn't a rigid requirement that must be proven in order to claim the tripel crown). Brewers can pretty much do what they want—and as long as they continue to give us delicious beer, we keep nodding along.

PILSNER

In general, **pilsners** are lagers. They are mild and carbonated, with a bit of hops and a bit of malt, and endlessly drinkable. First brewed in Plzeň in the 1840s in what was known at the time as Czechoslovakia, pilsners quickly became one of the most popular styles of the time and put lagers on the map. The brewery to brew the first pilsner is now known as

Pilsner Urquell and is still in operation and distribution today. Pilsners make an excellent gateway to craft beers for those hooked on the macro lager. They are usually lower in ABV, crisp, and clean.

BOCK

Bocks are the reason that people can't accurately say that lagers are low on flavor, a misconception that has darkened the lager's door for years. Also of German origin, modern bocks are dark, lively, and full of flavor without being overpowering. Think of what would happen if you crossed a brown ale with a pilsner, and you'll get the idea. They can also run around the spectrum a bit to give you the strength you want. A **doppelbock** is richer and higher in alcohol, while a **maibock** (also known as **helles bock** or **heller bock**) is on the other end of the spectrum, with a milder flavor and a lower alcohol content.

WILD ALE/SOUR

In the past decade, wild ales (also known as **sours**) have gone from almost nonexistent to a mainstay in every decent taproom in the nation. They're beers brewed with the yeast of the past. Years ago, before science could explain stuff to us, brewers didn't know *why* fermentation happened, only *that* it happened. For a while, the brewers of yesteryear would stir the mighty beer with a "magic" stick to make sure the mystifying bubbles would appear in the new batch of brew (and probably say a prayer or perform a chant to make sure it stuck). What they didn't know was that the stick wasn't magic at all; it was just transferring wild yeast that was already in the environment from one batch to another. Modern brewers have more precise techniques to get wild yeast into their beer (no magic sticks that I'm aware of, but probably plenty of prayers), but the flavors are much the same as in ancient ales. The flavor is decidedly sour, using much the same yeast and bacteria for flavor as sourdough bread. Common wild ales include **gose**, **lambic**, **gueuze** (a type of lambic), **Brett** (named after a wild yeast strain called *Brettanomyces*), **saison**, and **Flanders red**. Generally, the hop and malt profiles take a back seat to the yeast flavors, and they are most often well carbonated, making them great on a hot day. Sours tend to be perfect for that friend of yours who doesn't like craft beer but does like cider and white wine.

KÖLSCH

Kölsch is a great beer to make friends with. Remember our talk about ales versus lagers, and how the distinctions can be confusing? This is exhibit A: a kölsch is a lager, but it's made with ale yeast, so it's both an ale and a lager. First brewed in Cologne, Germany, it is in a lot of ways the best of both worlds. It's clean, crisp, light, and refreshing—you can't go wrong with a kölsch.

FRUIT AND VEGETABLE BEER

Fruit and vegetable beers are the core of seasonal beers, for the mere fact that they use in-season produce and are put out into the market alongside those same fruits and vegetables. Sure, you've heard of pumpkin beers, but there are so many more offerings. From peach to sweet potatoes, there isn't an edible plant that hasn't found its way into a beer somewhere in the world.

BARREL-AGED BEER

Barrel-aged beer is just what it sounds like: beer that has been aged in barrels. Traditionally, the beer chosen for the aging process was a stout or a porter. However, it's becoming increasingly common to venture away from those two—everything from IPAs to pilsners have been aged to stunning results. One of my favorite creations is the **barrel-aged sour**. Usually, the barrels have been previously used to age spirits, such as bourbon or rum (although wine, gin, and tequila barrels have hosted their fair share of beer over the years). Barreled beer is left in a cool, dry space for months, or even years, to continue to age, ferment, and mingle with the residue of the previous occupant in the wooden staves. These beers will continue to age well in their bottles (if cellared correctly), sometimes for decades. The process dramatically increases the ABV, often pushing it over 10 percent and even as high as 30 percent.

MEASURING BEER

While a standard pint glass is 16 ounces, a standard beer bottle or can is 12 ounces, and that gives you exactly 1½ cups of beer to use in your cooking. Very few recipes need exactly one bottle of beer, though, so here is a quick chart to make sure you have enough beer on hand before you start to cook.

Volume (US)	Volume (US)	Weight (Metric)
1 tablespoon	0.5 ounce	14 g
2 tablespoons	1 ounce	28 g
¼ cup	2 ounces	57 g
⅓ cup	2.6 ounces	74 g
½ cup	4 ounces	113 g
¾ cup	6 ounces	170 g
1 cup	8 ounces	227 g
1½ cups	12 ounces	340 g

SPRING

/ ˈspriŋ /

VERB: to leap or jump up suddenly

NOUN: a time or season of growth or development; specifically, the season between winter and summer

---

When I was in college, a history professor gave an entire lecture about the first day of spring, or the vernal equinox. He became animated, his hands waving wildly as he paced the room. He had theories, backed up with facts but not proven, that the Mayan temples had been built to celebrate that day, and even Stonehenge had been used as a site of vernal equinox festivities. The idea that this day, this marking of one season into the next, could have been the most important day of the year at one point in time stayed with me. I realized that I'd never really noted the first day of spring before—it wasn't as important as "the first day I didn't need a coat" or "the first day I could wear shorts," but the importance was undeniable. The ground was ready to be planted, and everyone was recovering from the harsh weather of winter and spilling into the preparation for summer. Spring is a period of revival, and a reminder that the best is yet to come.

SPRING PRODUCE

🌿 denotes vegan recipe or easy vegan adaptations given

APRICOTS

When I was a kid, we had an apricot tree in the backyard. When it came into season, it fruited with a vengeance. It was as if, all of a sudden, thousands of orange gems weighed down the branches. The race was on to use as many as we could before they left us to wait an entire year before they showed up again. When selecting your haul of apricots, look for fruit that has no bruises and is still fairly firm, as it will age well off the tree. Store apricots at room temperature until ripe, then transfer to the fridge until ready to use.

ARTICHOKES

Artichokes have my heart. Not just because they look like giant hop flowers, but also because they're an interactive food. They necessitate getting your hands dirty and digging in—I love them for that. To pick the best, look for tightly packed leaves; they'll start to drift farther from the center as they age off the plant. Also, you want 'em heavy. The freshest artichokes will be the heaviest for their size. Spritz the stem with water, then store in a plastic bag in the fridge for up to five days.

ASPARAGUS

I like them thick. For years people would tell you that thin was in, and that the fat ones weren't worth the oil you cooked them in. I'm here to tell you, my friends, that's just not true. Big is beautiful, and just as tender and flavorful—plus, a fat stalk is easier to peel, wrap, and slice. Look for asparagus that's firm, straight, and tight. Avoid stalks with wrinkles or dried ends.

BASIL

For the purposes of this book, I used good ol' standard Genovese basil, even though I think you should venture out. I mean, have you tried Thai basil? Or lemon basil? Did you know there is such a thing as purple basil or cinnamon basil? A pesto with purple basil or a lime curd with lemon basil sounds fantastic, doesn't it? Basil is best fresh from the ground, and therefore I recommend you start a little herb garden. Basil is nearly effortless to grow and maintain in season; just keep a small pot in direct sunlight in your kitchen window. Make sure to keep the soil moist and harvest leaves when you need them.

BEETS

Beets get a bad rap, and I blame whoever decided that canning them and forcing them on generations of children was a good idea. If you can't stand the red variety, give the golden guys a try. Golden beets are milder and sweeter and don't have the earthy flavor that's plagued the red beet since the dawn of the can opener. Look for a medium-size beet, avoiding any that are large or have a hairy root tip. Make sure the greens are bright and without any sign of wilting. Don't discard the greens; they make an excellent addition to salads or a replacement for the herb in your favorite pesto recipe.

ENGLISH PEAS

English peas are thrilling. When they come into season and I see them at the market for the first time, God help anyone in my path. I'll load up, happily shelling them, watching the pile of little green treasures grow in my bowl. I like them raw or lightly cooked; the crunch and flavor are delightful. Peas are best as soon as they're harvested, so store them in the fridge and plan to use them as quickly as you can.

KALE

Kale has one of the longest growing seasons of any vegetable, peaking in either the spring or summer months. Bookmark recipes you like, even when you want to cook only in-season produce; you'll get good use out of them. It's a rare month of the year when you won't be able to source kale, but spring is when all types of kale are at their most abundant. Look for bright, crispy leaves that show no signs of wilting. Store in the fridge, but make sure the leaves are free from moisture—that means opting to wash just before use rather than before storage.

MANGOES

Of the many varieties of mangoes, I favor red Tommy Atkins mangoes. They're the most widely available mangoes in the United States, and with a mildly tart sweetness and a firm but tender flesh, it's not hard to see why. If you favor a sweeter fruit, seek out the similar-looking but much sweeter Kent variety. Whichever mango you choose, look for one that gives just slightly when pressed, but not too much. You don't want it overripened.

STRAWBERRIES

It may be because of how much time I spent there, but I firmly believe that the best strawberries in the world are grown in California. They are even better enjoyed close to where they were farmed. If you're planning a visit to the Golden State anytime soon, make time for a trip to the farmers market, specifically to sample some strawberries. Although they come into peak season in the spring and summer, they're still growing through most of the year on the lower Left Coast. Look for strawberries that are firm and bright red, with no green or light spots and no signs of mold or weeping. Store in the fridge until ready to use.

SWISS CHARD

A cousin to cool kid kale, Swiss chard is just as fantastic and even more beautiful. I tend to prefer the milder flavors of chard to kale, and I often substitute it in recipes that call for kale. It takes slightly less time to cook. (Keep that in mind if you want to try that swap.) Swiss chard can go by many aliases, such as silver beet, perpetual spinach, beet spinach, seakale beet, and leaf beet. Much like kale, this is a green that can be grown year-round in most of the world but comes into peak abundance in late spring.

SPRING BEERS

As the weather warms and the ground thaws, the beer starts to change. The shift is small at first, as many breweries try to push the last of their winter ales out the door and prepare for the hoppy, fruity beers of summer. But because the season isn't so polarized by temperature extremes, the beer has some room to roam. This is also to say that spring beer is the least defined of all seasonal offerings. Possibly because our experience of "spring" is so different across the United States—from snowfall to triple-digit heat—there isn't a common shared experience of this seasons. However, in general, look for beers to become hoppier, more carbonated, and lighter in color than winter beers, but still with a pronounced malt profile.

 BARREL-AGED SOUR. Spring is the perfect time for these wild-fermented beers to make a splash on the scene. Their relatively high ABV and malt characteristics go well with weather that isn't too hot, but their crisp fruitiness is very welcome as the sun is starting to shine.

SAISON. Although historically these wild-fermented Belgian ales were saved until summer to consume, more recently the release of saisons occurs in the spring. The funky yeast it's brewed with gives a complex flavor, but the overall ABV is lower than most of the winter beer you've grown accustomed to.

 IMPERIAL IPA. Unlike the lower-alcohol session beers of summer, the spring IPAs tend to still be big in ABV like the winter beers, but with a strong hop bite like the summer beers.

BOCK. This lager looks darker than it tastes and offers up some nice carbonation. While these are beers that'll be around all year, spring is the perfect time of year for their clean, light, malty profiles. Expect notes of nuts, dark fruit, or caramel.

BELGIAN TRIPEL. The fact that this is such a broad category means that there is a Belgian ale for every season. Those that are still on the paler side, like the Belgian tripel, are perfect for spring. Tripels are straw colored, slightly higher in alcohol than other beers of that color, and full of malty sweetness. Although these beers look innocent with their golden color and thick, creamy head, they can be fierce. A nice carbonation level, flavors of fruit and bread, and a strong kick to the ABV make these the perfect beers to sip in the springtime.

PALE ALE. Pale ales are the backbone of most craft beer offerings and play well in all seasons. Think of pale ales like potatoes: you can get them and enjoy them around the calendar. They have enough malt to stand up to colder temperatures, as well as enough carbonation to handle the warmer months. (Beer, not potatoes, that is—if your potato is carbonated, you must reevaluate your produce selection process.) They are just as at home at an early winter football party as they are at a summer cookout, but spring is when they are ideal. The malt is present, as are the hops, and the ABV is fairly average.

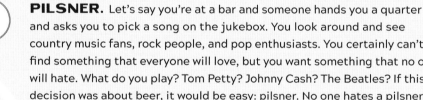

PILSNER. Let's say you're at a bar and someone hands you a quarter and asks you to pick a song on the jukebox. You look around and see country music fans, rock people, and pop enthusiasts. You certainly can't find something that everyone will love, but you want something that no one will hate. What do you play? Tom Petty? Johnny Cash? The Beatles? If this decision was about beer, it would be easy: pilsner. No one hates a pilsner. It's clean and crisp and has enough malt and hops, but not too much of either. It's a crowd-pleaser. It's perfect in the warmer months and can carry you from spring well into summer.

APRICOT, SERRANO, AND SOUR ALE JAM

MAKES 1 QUART

This isn't your basic sandwich jam, the type that makes its way into a hastily constructed lunch that spends half the day in a paper sack. Rather, it's the sort that takes up well-earned space on a cheese platter or adds a gourmet touch to panini. It's the kind that gets tucked into a gift basket next to aged cheese and great beer. Make a double batch—you'll figure out what to do with it. A sour ale, specifically a barrel-aged sour if you can get your hands on one, will bring a bright, funky, lively flavor that will highlight the sweet-tart flavors of the apricot and bring them to life. If you can't find a barrel-aged sour, look for a fruit sour (a sour ale that's been brewed with fruit).

3½ cups	pitted, chopped apricots (15–18)	680 g
1	serrano chile, seeded and finely chopped	
2 cups	granulated sugar	400 g
½ cup	sour ale	113 g
1 teaspoon	kosher salt	6 g

Combine all the ingredients in a stockpot and bring to a slow boil over medium-high heat. Cook, stirring frequently, until the mixture thickens, about 15 minutes. Allow to cool before using.

Store in an airtight container in the fridge for up to 2 weeks or can for shelf storage.

GRILLED APRICOT AND
SAISON SHORTCAKES
WITH GINGER MASCARPONE WHIPPED CREAM

SERVES 8

It's no coincidence that grilling season starts just as apricots start to show their gloriously fuzzy little faces at the farmers markets. The smoky char of the grill paired with the familiar, sweet tang of these delicious little fruits will make you wonder if you'll ever be able to enjoy apricots without a quick trip to the grates of a hot grill first. Serve this with the saison you made it with, or pair it with a slightly hoppy pilsner for a contrast of complementary flavors. Add whipped mascarpone, and you'll be a believer in the power of grilled fruit.

SHORTCAKES

3½ cups	all-purpose flour	420 g
1 teaspoon	baking powder	4 g
1 teaspoon	baking soda	6 g
½ teaspoon	kosher salt	3 g
¼ cup	granulated sugar	50 g
1 stick	unsalted butter, chilled and cubed	114 g
¾ cup	saison	170 g
⅓ cup	buttermilk	74 g

FILLING

12–16	ripe apricots, halved and pitted	
1 tablespoon, packed	golden brown sugar	14 g
8 ounces	mascarpone	227 g
1 cup	heavy cream	240 g
¼ cup	powdered sugar	30 g
1 teaspoon	pure vanilla extract	5 g
¼ teaspoon	finely grated fresh ginger	1 g

TO MAKE THE SHORTCAKES: Preheat the oven to 425°F. Line a rimmed baking sheet with parchment paper.

Combine the flour, baking powder, baking soda, salt, and sugar in the bowl of a food processor and pulse to mix. Add the butter and process until well combined. Add the beer and buttermilk and process until the dough just comes together.

Drop ¼-cup mounds of dough onto the prepared baking sheet, spacing them evenly.

Bake for 10 to 12 minutes, until the shortcakes are lightly golden brown and cooked through. Transfer them to a wire rack and allow to cool.

TO MAKE THE FILLING: Prepare a charcoal grill for direct heat or heat a gas grill to medium-high.

Place the apricot halves, cut side down, on the cooking grate. Grill until grill marks appear, about 3 minutes. Remove the apricots from the grill and slice them thinly lengthwise. Transfer the apricot slices to a bowl and sprinkle them with the brown sugar, tossing to coat.

In the bowl of a stand mixer fitted with the whisk attachment, beat the mascarpone on medium-high speed until light and fluffy. Add the heavy cream and beat on high until soft peaks form. Add the powdered sugar, vanilla, and ginger and beat on medium-low to combine.

To assemble, split the shortcakes. Fill each with mascarpone whipped cream and apricot slices. Serve.

BEER-BRAISED ARTICHOKES WRAPPED IN PUFF PASTRY

I'm not sure what I expected, but the first time I saw an artichoke bush it took me a bit by surprise. You mean, it's just sticking out of that plant? Like a large green flower? They look like fat green pine cones, like absurdly large hop flowers, like something that should be high in the air and hanging down and mocking me, out of reach. But they're well within reach, and perfect with a pilsner.

2	**large artichokes**	
3 tablespoons	**unsalted butter**	42 g
1 teaspoon	**kosher salt**	6 g
2	**large cloves garlic, grated**	
3 cups	**pilsner**	680 g
for dusting	**all-purpose flour**	
1 (8-ounce) sheet	**puff pastry, chilled but not frozen**	
2 tablespoons	**unsalted butter, melted**	28 g

Trim 1 to 2 inches from the top of each artichoke. Remove and discard several outer layers of leaves until the leaves start to get thinner and lighter in color. Halve the artichokes lengthwise. Using a melon baller or grapefruit spoon, remove and discard the inner chokes (the fuzzy centers). Cut each half crosswise into 1½-inch slices. You should get about three slices from each half.

In a large Dutch oven, melt the butter over high heat. Stir in the salt and garlic. Add the artichoke slices and cook until browned on both sides, about 3 minutes per side.

Add the beer, cover, reduce the heat to medium-low, and simmer for 45 minutes. Remove the artichoke slices with a slotted spoon and transfer to paper towels to drain and dry.

Preheat the oven to 425°F. Line a rimmed baking sheet with parchment paper.

Flour a clean, dry work surface. Roll out the puff pastry into a 12 × 16-inch rectangle. Cut it crosswise into strips that are about 1 inch wide; you will need as many strips as you have artichoke slices. Work quickly to keep the puff pastry from warming up too much.

One at a time, wrap a strip of puff pastry around a slice of artichoke, leaving the top ½ inch of the leaves sticking out. Place on the prepared baking sheet. Brush each wrapped artichoke with some melted butter.

Bake for 12 to 15 minutes, until the puff pastry is golden brown.

To eat, use the exposed artichoke leaves as a handle. Eat the pastry-covered portion and discard the leaves.

BEER-STEAMED ARTICHOKES
WITH ROASTED GARLIC HUMMUS

SERVES 4

This is the perfect dish to make for that certain someone whom you adore but don't want to make out with. It's an "I want to spend a lot of time not kissing you" sort of recipe. You and said not-kissing friend will spend a lovely afternoon splitting a few good beers and devouring this platter. And after consuming the entire head of roasted garlic called for in this recipe, neither of you will be tempted to change the status of your relationship.

1	**large head garlic**	
4 tablespoons, divided, + more to taste	**extra virgin olive oil**	60+ g
2	**large artichokes**	
2–3 cups	**bock**	454–680 g
1 (15-ounce) can	**chickpeas, rinsed and drained**	425 g
3 tablespoons	**tahini**	42 g
¼ cup	**imperial IPA**	57 g
½ teaspoon + more to taste	**kosher salt**	3+ g

Preheat the oven to 425°F.

Remove most of the outer papery skin from the head of garlic. Trim off about ¼ inch from the top of the head to expose all the cloves while keeping the head intact. Place on a square of aluminum foil. Drizzle with 1 tablespoon (15 g) of the olive oil and close the foil tightly around the garlic.

Place the wrapped garlic on a rimmed baking sheet or in a baking dish and roast until softened, about 40 minutes. Set the garlic aside, still wrapped, to cool.

While the garlic is roasting, prepare the artichokes. Trim 1 to 2 inches from the top of each artichoke. Remove and discard several outer layers of leaves until the leaves start to get thinner and lighter in color. Halve the artichokes lengthwise. Using a melon baller or grapefruit spoon, remove and discard the inner chokes (the fuzzy centers).

Put the artichokes, cut side down, in a large Dutch oven or stockpot and pour in enough of the bock to come about halfway up the sides of the artichokes. Cover the pot and bring the beer to a simmer over medium-high heat. Cook until the leaves can be removed easily from the artichokes, about 30 minutes. Throughout the cooking time, check the pot to make sure it isn't dry, adding more beer when necessary to maintain a liquid level about halfway up the sides of the artichokes. Use a slotted spoon to transfer the artichokes to a serving dish to cool slightly.

When the garlic is cool, make the hummus. One at a time, gently pinch the chickpeas to remove and discard the thin, translucent skins. (This will help ensure a truly creamy hummus.) Combine the chickpeas, tahini, imperial IPA, salt, and remaining 3 tablespoons (45 g) of olive oil in a blender or the bowl of a food processor. Unwrap the roasted garlic and gently squeeze the head over the blender so that the soft cloves drop in.

Process the mixture until smooth. Taste and add salt as needed. Add more olive oil for a creamier texture as desired.

Pull the leaves off the artichokes and dip them into the hummus. To eat, scrape the hummus and the meat of the artichoke off the leaves with your teeth.

PAN-SEARED ASPARAGUS
WITH POACHED EGG AND BEER BÉARNAISE SAUCE

SERVES 4

Right out of college, I worked as a social worker for gang members in the inner city of Los Angeles. One day, for a company potluck, I brought asparagus, pan-seared in herb butter. At first, it was side-eyed by the other social workers—passed up for sweet potatoes, greens, and mac and cheese. Then, as the other offerings began to dwindle, brave souls began to give it a go. Another social worker, a Los Angeles native, admitted he'd never had asparagus before and ended up asking for the recipe. "I just . . . never thought anything that looked like an unripened pencil," he said, "could actually taste good." Add the creamy, rich, beautiful taste of a French butter sauce, and it can even make you want to eat that pencil.

¼ cup	pale ale	57 g
2 tablespoons	white wine vinegar	30 g
1 tablespoon	chopped shallot	8 g
2 tablespoons	fresh tarragon leaves	3 g
1 tablespoon	fresh chervil leaves	1.5 g
3	large egg yolks	
1 teaspoon, divided	kosher salt	6 g
1 stick	unsalted butter	114 g
2 tablespoons	extra virgin olive oil	30 g
15–18	thick asparagus spears, trimmed	
½ teaspoon	freshly ground black pepper	1 g
4	large eggs, poached (see Note)	

Combine the beer, vinegar, shallot, tarragon, and chervil in a small saucepan. Cook over medium-high heat until reduced by about half, about 6 minutes.

Transfer the beer mixture to a blender and let cool for a few minutes. Add the egg yolks and ½ teaspoon (3 g) of the salt. Blend on high for 3 minutes.

Wipe out the saucepan and melt the butter over medium-high heat. Remove the circular cap from the blender lid. With the blender running on high, slowly pour in the hot butter in a steady stream. After all the butter has been added, continue to blend on high for 2 more minutes. The béarnaise sauce should resemble slightly thin mayonnaise.

Heat the olive oil in a skillet over medium-high heat. Add the asparagus and season with the remaining ½ teaspoon (3 g) of salt. Cook, rolling the asparagus back and forth in the pan occasionally, until the asparagus spears start to brown and soften but are still firm.

Divide the asparagus among four plates. Drizzle with the béarnaise sauce and top each with a poached egg. Serve.

NOTE

Poaching eggs is a great skill to have in the kitchen, but don't expect to get it right the first time. It takes some practice! In a wide sauté pan, bring about 5 inches of water and a splash of white vinegar to a low simmer (don't boil!). Crack each egg into a small prep dish or ramekin. One by one, gently slide each egg from its dish into the pot, making sure they aren't touching. Cook for 3 to 4 minutes, until the whites have set but the yolks are still runny. Remove each egg with a slotted spoon and drain briefly on a paper towel before plating.

SHAVED ASPARAGUS SALAD
WITH LEMON-PILSNER VINAIGRETTE

SERVES 4

This salad terrifies me. Not so much the salad, per se, but the fact that it necessitates the use of a vegetable peeler. Years ago, I was a finalist in a timed cooking contest at the Culinary Institute of America in Northern California. My first task was to peel cucumbers. When the bell sounded and time started, I was off! My first swipe with the peeler landed squarely on my thumb. It forced me to step away, bandage and finger-cot myself, and lose 10 minutes. Ever since, vegetable peelers terrify me. I say this to you to affirm that even I, with my inept motor skills and clumsy peeling, am still able to make this beautiful salad without incident. To be honest, it is so good that even a small injury would still be worth it.

SALAD

15–18	thick asparagus spears	
3 cups	baby arugula	85 g
¾ cup	chopped roasted hazelnuts (see Note)	102 g
¼ cup	shaved Parmigiano-Reggiano	28 g

VINAIGRETTE

¼ cup	extra virgin olive oil	60 g
2 tablespoons	freshly squeezed lemon juice	27 g
2 tablespoons	pilsner	30 g
2 teaspoons	honey	14 g
1 teaspoon	whole-grain Dijon mustard	8 g
1 teaspoon	freshly ground black pepper	2 g

TO MAKE THE SALAD: One at a time, grab the bottom of an asparagus spear (the bottom 2 inches that would otherwise be trimmed away) and shave thin ribbons down the length of the spear and the tip with a vegetable peeler. Discard the bottom portion. Repeat this process for all the spears.

On a serving platter, toss together the shaved asparagus, arugula, hazelnuts, and Parmigiano-Reggiano.

TO MAKE THE VINAIGRETTE: In a small bowl, whisk together the olive oil, lemon juice, beer, honey, mustard, and pepper. Drizzle the dressing over the salad just before serving.

NOTE

You can purchase roasted hazelnuts, but you can also roast your own at home. Just preheat the oven to 300°F, spread out the nuts on a rimmed baking sheet, and roast them for 15 minutes, tossing once during cooking. Keep a close eye on them—nuts can scorch quickly!

BASIL AND BELGIAN ALE LIME CURD TART
WITH TRIPEL WHIPPED CREAM

SERVES 6

*It's not uncommon that I'm asked to bring a dessert to a dinner party. The host has enough to do—
who needs to spend time worrying about what to eat when the meal is over? Tarts are the perfect
dinner party dessert. They look beautiful, are best made in advance, transport fairly well, and can
be filled with nearly anything. Like beer-flavored things. People love beer-flavored things.*

CRUST

1½ cups + more for dusting	all-purpose flour	180+ g
1 teaspoon	kosher salt	6 g
2 tablespoons	granulated sugar	26 g
1 stick	unsalted butter, softened	114 g
3 tablespoons	unsalted butter, chilled and cut into small cubes	42 g
¼ cup	Belgian tripel	57 g

FILLING

1	large egg	
3	large egg yolks	
1¼ cups	granulated sugar	250 g
1 tablespoon	grated lime zest	6 g
¾ cup	freshly squeezed lime juice	178 g
1 tablespoon	chopped fresh basil leaves	3 g
½ cup	Belgian tripel	113 g
1 tablespoon	cornstarch	11 g
1 stick	unsalted butter, cut into cubes	114 g

WHIPPED CREAM

1 cup	heavy cream	240 g
3 tablespoons	powdered sugar	22 g
2 tablespoons	barrel-aged sour	28 g

TO MAKE THE CRUST: Combine the flour, salt, sugar, and softened butter in the bowl of a food processor. Process until the mixture is combined. Add the cold butter and pulse until the mixture is just combined. You will still be able to see some larger pieces of butter, which will create flaky layers. Pulse in the beer until it is completely incorporated. The dough will be very soft.

Lay a long sheet of plastic wrap on a work surface. Turn out the dough onto the plastic wrap. Form the dough into a disk about 6 inches in diameter and wrap it tightly in the plastic. Refrigerate until firm, at least 3 hours and up to 3 days.

Preheat the oven to 350°F.

Lightly flour a clean, dry work surface. Roll out the tart dough until it is about 12 inches in diameter and about ¼ inch thick. Line a 9-inch tart pan with the dough. Prick the bottom of the dough several times with a fork to release air bubbles during baking, then add pie weights or dried beans if desired. (Pie weights will help the pie crust keep its shape.)

Bake until the crust is lightly golden brown, 15 to 18 minutes. Remove the tart pan from the oven and set it aside to cool.

RECIPE CONTINUES ☞

BASIL AND BELGIAN ALE
LIME CURD TART WITH TRIPEL
WHIPPED CREAM

CONTINUED

TO MAKE THE FILLING: In a small saucepan, whisk together the whole egg and egg yolks, sugar, lime zest and juice, basil, beer, and cornstarch. Add the butter cubes. Place the pan over medium heat and cook, whisking frequently, until the butter has melted and the mixture has thickened, about 12 minutes.

Pour the filling into the tart crust and smooth the top. Transfer the tart to the refrigerator and chill until set, at least 2 hours and up to 24 hours. Remove the tart from the pan and transfer it to a serving platter.

TO MAKE THE WHIPPED CREAM: Combine the cream and powdered sugar in the bowl of a stand mixer fitted with the whisk attachment. Whip the mixture on medium-high speed until soft peaks form. With the mixer running, slowly pour in the beer until just combined and soft peaks return.

Top the tart with the whipped cream just before serving. If making in advance, store the whipped cream in an airtight container in the refrigerator for up to 24 hours.

BASIL, PECAN, AND SAISON PESTO

Pesto is one of my favorite DIY food gifts. It's the perfect way to give a little piece of the season to someone hosting you for dinner. Feel free to mix it up a little by substituting some parsley or cilantro for a portion of the basil, using walnuts instead of pecans, or swapping in a different beer. Just make sure it's a beer you like, as you'll have to "figure out" what to do with the remaining cup and a quarter of beer in the bottle. Sorry about that.

½ cup	chopped pecans	68 g
½ cup	grated Parmigiano-Reggiano	56 g
3 cups, packed	fresh basil leaves	48 g
2	cloves garlic, peeled and lightly smashed	
1 teaspoon	kosher salt	6 g
½ teaspoon	freshly ground black pepper	1 g
⅓ cup	extra virgin olive oil	80 g
¼ cup	saison	57 g

Put the pecans in a small skillet and toss over high heat until lightly toasted, about 5 minutes. Watch them carefully, as they burn quickly.

Transfer the toasted pecans to the bowl of a food processor and add the Parmigiano-Reggiano, basil, garlic, salt, and pepper. Process until only small crumbs remain.

With the food processor running, slowly pour in the olive oil through the feed tube. Then, add the beer in a slow, steady stream until the pesto is well combined. Store in an airtight container in the refrigerator for up to 1 week.

SALT-ROASTED GOLDEN BEETS
WITH WHIPPED BELGIAN ALE MASCARPONE
AND HERB GREMOLATA

SERVES 4

I got married earlier this year, and we served a version of this dish at the wedding. This was mostly because my new husband wanted to tell the story of the first time I made it for him, and the horror he felt when I first mentioned wanting to make beets. "Thing was," he told our guests, "I really wanted to see her naked later. So when she said she was making beets—and I have a well-documented, abject hatred for beets—I decided just to grin and bear it. But the thing I've learned about Jackie's cooking is that she can make anything taste amazing. And these beets were fantastic. I didn't just have to deal with them, I completely fell in love with them." If these beets made him a believer, they can turn any beet-hater around.

3–4	large golden beets	
1 pound	kosher salt	454 g
2	cloves garlic, peeled	
3 tablespoons	chopped fresh flat-leaf parsley leaves	3 g
1 tablespoon	chopped fresh chives	1 g
1 tablespoon	chopped fresh basil leaves	1 g
3 tablespoons	extra virgin olive oil	45 g
8 ounces	mascarpone	227 g
3 tablespoons	heavy cream	45 g
3 tablespoons	Belgian tripel	43 g

Preheat the oven to 425°F.

Choose a loaf pan or small, deep baking dish that will just fit the beets without the beets touching the sides or each other. Pour a thin layer of salt into the pan. Place the beets on top and completely cover them with the remaining salt.

Cover the pan with aluminum foil and bake for 45 minutes to 2 hours, until a fork easily pierces the beets through the salt. Remove the pan from the oven, remove the foil, and set the pan aside until the beets are cool enough to handle.

To blanch the garlic and mellow the flavor, bring a small saucepan of water to a boil over high heat. Drop the garlic cloves into the boiling water and boil for 1 minute. Remove the garlic cloves with a slotted spoon and immediately plunge them into a bowl filled with ice and water. Transfer the garlic to a cutting board, mince it, and put it in a small bowl. Add the parsley, chives, basil, and olive oil and stir to combine. Set the gremolata aside.

In the bowl of a stand mixer fitted with the paddle attachment, beat the mascarpone on medium-high speed until light and fluffy. With the machine running, slowly add the cream and beer until they are completely incorporated.

Once the beets have cooled, remove them from the pan, brushing away all the salt. Rub the beets with your hands or a clean, dry towel until all the skin comes off; discard the skin. Cut the beets crosswise into ½-inch-thick slices. Arrange them in concentric circles on a serving platter. Top with the whipped mascarpone, drizzle with the gremolata, and serve.

CHOCOLATE-HAZELNUT BEET MUFFINS

Sure, it's beer and chocolate, but it's also vegetables and protein! It's (sorta) healthy and completely appropriate for breakfast, even though it tastes like a cupcake that someone forgot to frost. Side note: replace the nuts with chocolate chips and add frosting, and you can eat beer cupcakes for breakfast.

1	large red beet, quartered	
1½ cups	all-purpose flour	180 g
⅓ cup	unsweetened cocoa powder	60 g
1 cup	granulated sugar	200 g
1 teaspoon	baking soda	6 g
1 teaspoon	baking powder	4 g
1 teaspoon	kosher salt	6 g
1 teaspoon	espresso powder	1 g
½ cup	bock	113 g
⅓ cup	coconut oil, melted	74 g
1 teaspoon	pure vanilla extract	5 g
½ cup	chopped hazelnuts	68 g

Bring a small pot of salted water to a boil over high heat. Add the beet and boil until a fork easily pierces the beet, about 20 minutes. Drain the beet and set it aside until it is cool enough to handle. Rub the beet with your hands or a clean, dry towel until all the skin comes off; discard the skin. Transfer the beet to a high-powered blender or the bowl of a food processor and purée. Measure out 1 cup (165 g) of the beet purée and reserve the rest for another use.

Preheat the oven to 350°F. Grease a 12-cup muffin tin.

In a bowl, whisk together the flour, cocoa powder, sugar, baking soda, baking powder, salt, and espresso powder.

Make a well in the center of the flour mixture. Add the beet purée, beer, coconut oil, vanilla, and hazelnuts to the well, then stir until everything is just combined. Be careful not to overmix.

Fill each cup of the prepared muffin tin about two-thirds of the way with batter.

Bake for 18 to 20 minutes, until the tops spring back when lightly touched. Set the muffin tin on a rack to cool before removing the muffins and serving.

ENGLISH PEA AND BOCK RISOTTO

SERVES 4

The first time I made risotto, I used a recipe off the back of a bag of Arborio rice. I decided that if some cheese and butter was good, then more had to be better. It was rich, creamy, and flavorful—I was hooked. The bright freshness of newly shelled English peas adds a beautiful contrast to the richness of the risotto. Here, the beer replaces the traditional white wine, giving the risotto just a hint of beautiful malty flavor.

RISOTTO

2½ cups	reduced-sodium vegetable broth	567 g
2 tablespoons	unsalted butter	28 g
1 tablespoon	chopped shallot	8 g
2	cloves garlic, minced	
¾ cup	Arborio rice	150 g
2 tablespoons	extra virgin olive oil	30 g
½ cup + 2 tablespoons, divided	bock	142 g
¼ cup	grated Parmigiano-Reggiano	28 g
2 tablespoons	heavy cream	30 g
¼ teaspoon	kosher salt	1.5 g
½ teaspoon	freshly ground black pepper	1 g

PEAS

2 tablespoons	unsalted butter	28 g
1¼ cups	shelled fresh English peas	200 g
½ teaspoon	kosher salt	3 g
½ teaspoon	freshly ground black pepper	2 g
½ teaspoon	garlic powder	2 g
1 teaspoon	freshly squeezed lemon juice	5 g

TO MAKE THE RISOTTO: In a small saucepan, bring the broth to a simmer over medium-low heat. Throughout the process, you want to keep it just simmering, but not boiling. Adjust the heat level as needed.

In a medium saucepan, melt the butter over medium heat. Add the shallot and cook, stirring frequently, for 5 minutes, or until softened but not browned. Add the garlic and cook until you can smell it, about 20 seconds.

Stir in the rice and olive oil and cook for 2 minutes, or until the rice is completely coated and smells slightly nutty. Do not allow the rice to brown.

Add ½ cup (113 g) of the beer and cook, stirring frequently, until the rice has absorbed the liquid and the pan begins to dry. Add about ½ cup (113 g) of the warm broth. Cook, stirring frequently, until the rice has absorbed most of the liquid, then add another ½ cup (113 g) of the broth. Repeat this process for about 20 minutes, until the rice is thick and cooked through. (Taste it and make sure it is not crunchy.) Don't leave the risotto while it's cooking, and be sure to stir frequently, as rice on the bottom of the pan burns easily. If you run out of broth, use hot water the same way you used the broth.

Reduce the heat to low and add the cheese, cream, and remaining 2 tablespoons (29 g) of beer. Season with the salt and pepper. The risotto should be soft and wet, not dry like regular rice. It should be firm enough to be served as a side on a plate, but soft enough to jiggle when the plate is shaken.

TO MAKE THE PEAS: Melt the butter in a skillet over medium-high heat. Add the peas, salt, pepper, garlic powder, and lemon juice. Cook, stirring occasionally, until the peas have softened, about 8 minutes. Plate the risotto, top with the peas, and serve warm.

**ENGLISH PEA
AND PILSNER
CREPES**

PAGE 56

ENGLISH PEA AND PILSNER CREPES
WITH BURRATA AND TOMATOES

I was in Tamarindo, Costa Rica, this year for a few hot days when I stumbled into a creperie off the beaten path. Since a beach town in Central America doesn't exactly scream "authentic French cuisine," I was skeptical. But several locals raved about it, and I was hungry. I ordered a savory crepe with burrata cheese, and it was the best decision I'd made in months. The owner—with a very authentic French accent—served it to me and confirmed that she was, in fact, a real-deal French chef. Turns out, you can *get French cuisine in Central America, and it's outstanding.*

CREPES

2	large eggs	
¾ cup	pilsner	170 g
½ cup	whole milk	120 g
1 cup	all-purpose flour	120 g
½ teaspoon	kosher salt	3 g
3 tablespoons + more as needed	unsalted butter, melted	42+ g
1 tablespoon	unsalted butter	14 g

FILLING

2 tablespoons	unsalted butter	28 g
1 cup	shelled fresh English peas	170 g
1 tablespoon	freshly squeezed lemon juice	18 g
½ teaspoon	kosher salt	3 g
1 tablespoon	chopped fresh basil leaves	1 g
1	large heirloom tomato, diced	
8 ounces	burrata	227 g

TO MAKE THE CREPES: Combine the eggs, beer, milk, flour, salt, and melted butter in a blender. Blend until combined. Cover and refrigerate for at least 1 hour and up to 12 hours.

In a 10-inch nonstick skillet, melt the butter over medium heat. Add about ¼ cup of the batter, swirling the pan to spread the batter into a thin circle. Allow to cook until the top is dry, about 3 minutes. Using a spatula, flip the crepe, then cook the other side until it is golden brown, about 3 minutes. Transfer the crepe to a plate. Repeat this process until all the batter is used, using additional melted butter if the crepes start to stick during cooking.

TO MAKE THE FILLING: Melt the butter in a skillet over medium-high heat. Add the peas and cook, stirring occasionally, until they are warm and just starting to wrinkle, about 6 minutes. Transfer the peas to a serving bowl. Add the lemon juice, salt, basil, and tomato and toss gently to combine.

Serve the crepes alongside the burrata and pea mixture, allowing guests to fill as desired.

KALE PANZANELLA
WITH TOASTED BEER BREAD

SERVES 4

I have nothing other than a hunch and my own intuition to assume that panzanella is what happened years ago when someone wanted a fresh summer salad but also wanted bread, or maybe even some Thanksgiving stuffing. It's the glorious meeting of all the delicious flavors of a bread stuffing, but with the bright freshness of a summer salad. It's a win-win. You can make the bread several days in advance.

3 cups	**all-purpose flour**	360 g
2 teaspoons	**baking powder**	8 g
2 teaspoons	**baking soda**	12 g
2 tablespoons, packed	**golden brown sugar**	24 g
1½ cups	**pilsner**	340 g
4 tablespoons	**unsalted butter, melted**	56 g
4 tablespoons, divided, + more for serving	**extra virgin olive oil**	60+ g
12–15	**thick asparagus spears, trimmed and chopped**	
2 cups	**chopped lacinato kale**	85 g
½ teaspoon	**kosher salt**	3 g
½ teaspoon	**freshly ground black pepper**	2 g
1–2	**large heirloom tomatoes, chopped**	
¾ cup	**shaved Parmigiano-Reggiano**	85 g
for serving	**balsamic glaze**	

Preheat the oven to 400°F. Grease an 8.5 × 4.5-inch loaf pan.

In a large bowl, whisk together the flour, baking powder, baking soda, brown sugar, and beer. Pour the batter into the prepared pan, then pour the melted butter over the batter.

Bake until the loaf is golden brown, about 40 minutes. Remove the bread from the oven and allow to cool. Cut the bread into small cubes.

Scatter the bread cubes on a rimmed baking sheet and drizzle with 2 tablespoons (30 g) of the olive oil. Bake until the bread cubes have toasted, about 15 minutes. Remove them from the oven.

In a skillet, heat the remaining 2 tablespoons (30 g) of olive oil over medium-high heat. Add the asparagus and kale and cook, stirring, until the vegetables have just softened, about 5 minutes. Season with the salt and pepper.

In a serving bowl, toss together the toasted bread, tomatoes, kale, asparagus, and Parmigiano-Reggiano. Drizzle with olive oil and balsamic glaze as desired. Serve immediately.

KALE AND
BELGIAN
ALE RICOTTA
MANICOTTI

PAGE 62

KALE AND BELGIAN ALE RICOTTA MANICOTTI

If you have yet to jump on the "make ricotta from scratch" train, here's your boarding call. It really is so simple—a few quick steps and you have your own batch of homemade ricotta cheese. It sounds like a feat of culinary wizardry, but it's not much more difficult than boiling pasta. Trust me, it's the least amount of effort you can put in to feel like a superhero.

RICOTTA

3 cups	whole milk (not ultra-pasteurized)	720 g
1 cup	heavy cream	240 g
½ teaspoon	kosher salt	3 g
⅓ cup + 2 tablespoons, divided	Belgian tripel	102 g
3 tablespoons	apple cider vinegar, freshly squeezed lemon juice, or a combination	45 g

TOMATO SAUCE

1 (28-ounce) can	diced tomatoes, drained	480 g
¼ cup	tomato paste	66 g
1 tablespoon	dried oregano	9 g
1 tablespoon	dried thyme	9 g
1 teaspoon	garlic powder	3 g
½ teaspoon	kosher salt	3 g
½ teaspoon	freshly ground black pepper	2 g
⅓ cup	Belgian tripel	74 g

MANICOTTI

8	manicotti shells	
2 tablespoons	extra virgin olive oil	30 g
¼ cup	chopped shallot	32 g
4 cups	chopped red kale	70 g
1 tablespoon	chopped fresh oregano leaves	3 g
½ teaspoon	kosher salt	3 g
2	cloves garlic, chopped	
1½ cups, divided	shaved Parmigiano-Reggiano	168 g

TO MAKE THE RICOTTA: In a stainless steel or enameled cast iron pot (not an aluminum pot), combine the milk, cream, salt, and ⅓ cup (74 g) of the beer. Clip a cooking thermometer onto the side of the pan. Turn the heat to medium-high and bring the liquid to 190°F, stirring occasionally to prevent the bottom from scorching. Keep a close eye on it. The liquid reaches and passes 190°F very quickly, and you don't want it rising above 200°F.

Remove the pot from the heat. Add the remaining 2 tablespoons (28 g) of beer and the vinegar and stir gently once or twice. It should curdle immediately. Allow the mixture to sit undisturbed for about 5 minutes.

Line a large strainer with one or two layers of cheesecloth. Set the strainer over a large bowl and place it in the sink.

Pour the ricotta into the strainer and allow to drain for 15 to 60 minutes, depending on your desired consistency. After 15 minutes, the ricotta will be a smooth, creamy, spreadable cheese. If you continue to allow it to drain, it will become firmer. It will also continue to firm once it is chilled, so be sure to remove it from the strainer *before* it reaches your desired level of firmness.

Store the ricotta in an airtight container in the refrigerator for up to 5 days.

TO MAKE THE TOMATO SAUCE: In a medium saucepan, combine the diced tomatoes, tomato paste, oregano, thyme, garlic powder, salt, pepper, and beer. Bring the mixture to a simmer over medium heat and cook, stirring occasionally, until thickened, about 15 minutes. Taste and adjust the seasoning as needed. (The tomato sauce can be made in advance and stored in an airtight container in the refrigerator for up to 5 days.)

TO MAKE THE MANICOTTI: Preheat the oven to 350°F.

Bring a large pot of salted water to a boil over high heat. Add the manicotti and cook until just before al dente, about 6 minutes. Drain.

In a skillet, heat the olive oil over medium heat. Add the shallot and cook for about 5 minutes, until just starting to brown. Stir in the kale, oregano, and salt and cook until the kale has softened. Stir in the garlic and cook for about 30 seconds.

Remove the skillet from the heat. Stir in the ricotta and 1 cup (112 g) of the Parmigiano-Reggiano. Transfer the mixture to a piping bag or a zip-top bag with a bottom corner cut off.

Pipe the filling into the manicotti. Arrange the stuffed manicotti tightly in a 7 × 11-inch baking dish. Cover them with the tomato sauce and top with the remaining ½ cup (56 g) of Parmigiano-Reggiano. Bake until the cheese has melted and the manicotti are warmed through, about 20 minutes. Serve warm.

MANGO-COCONUT IPA ICE CREAM

The first time I served this ice cream was at a dinner party. The brightness of the mango against the creamy coconut and pop of hops from the IPA was otherworldly. A friend of mine who can't eat dairy immediately threw her spoon down after the first bite: "I can't eat this." Confused, I asked why. "I can't eat dairy, and this obviously has a lot of it." I showed her the ingredients and told her to immediately go out and buy an ice cream maker and cases of coconut milk, because once you start making coconut ice cream, it's nearly impossible to stop. She texted me a week later: "Ice cream maker has been secured, batch number three underway."

1 (13.5-ounce) can	**full-fat coconut milk**	405 g
½ cup	**imperial IPA**	113 g
1	**large red mango, peeled, pitted, and diced**	
2 cups	**powdered sugar**	240 g
½ teaspoon	**kosher salt**	3 g
½ teaspoon	**pure vanilla extract**	2.5 g

Combine all the ingredients in a blender. Blend on high until the mixture is smooth. Transfer the ice cream base to an airtight container and refrigerate until chilled, about 1 hour.

Churn the ice cream base in an ice cream maker according to the manufacturer's instructions. Transfer the ice cream to a freezer-safe bowl and freeze until set, about 2 hours. Store in an airtight container in the freezer for up to 1 week.

MANGO SPRING ROLLS
WITH BELGIAN ALE AND PEANUT DIPPING SAUCE

I have a feeling that spring rolls were so named because the amazing abundance of fruit and herbs that come into season makes the perfect filling for these beautiful little handheld treats. Sure, you can make them all year long with a myriad of ingredients, but the beauty of spring produce just makes them pop. Feel free to play around with the ingredients, adding the ones you love and have access to—this is a recipe that takes well to adaptation and customization.

12 (8.5-inch) round sheets	rice paper	
2	large red mangoes, peeled, pitted, and thinly sliced	
1	large red bell pepper, seeded and thinly sliced	
1	large avocado, peeled, pitted, and sliced	
2 ounces	rice stick noodles (vermicelli), cooked according to package directions	57 g
¼ cup	chopped fresh cilantro leaves	6 g
for serving	Belgian Ale and Peanut Dipping Sauce (recipe follows)	

Pour ½ inch of water into a pie plate or wide, shallow bowl. One at a time, dunk a sheet of rice paper in the water, allowing it to soak until slightly softened, about 3 seconds. (The rice paper continues to soften as it sits.) Remove the rice paper from the water and place it on a flat glass or ceramic plate.

Working with one rice paper sheet at a time, place some of the mango, bell pepper, avocado, rice noodles, and cilantro in a long row down the center. Fold the edges of the rice paper in over the short sides of the filling, then tightly roll the rice paper lengthwise, forming a spring roll. Repeat this process with the remaining ingredients. Chill the spring rolls until ready to serve, up to 1 day. Serve with the dipping sauce on the side.

≫ BELGIAN ALE AND PEANUT DIPPING SAUCE ≪

¾ cup	creamy peanut butter	192 g
⅓ cup + more if needed	Belgian tripel	74+ g
3 tablespoons	reduced-sodium soy sauce	45 g
2 tablespoons	freshly squeezed lime juice	28 g
2 tablespoons	mirin	28 g
1 tablespoon	white vinegar	15 g
1 tablespoon	toasted sesame oil	15 g
1 tablespoon	sambal oelek (see Note)	15 g
1 tablespoon, packed	golden brown sugar	14 g
1 teaspoon	red pepper flakes	3 g

Combine all the ingredients in a small blender or the bowl of a food processor and blend until smooth. Thin with more beer, if desired. Use right away or store in an airtight container in the refrigerator for up to 5 days.

NOTE

Sambal oelek is a wonderful condiment to keep on hand. It's a beautiful Indonesian chili sauce, perfect for so many applications and a great way to make a dish taste like you used fresh chilies even when they aren't in season. Look for it in the Asian food section of most grocery stores.

STRAWBERRY-
COCONUT
LOAF CAKE

PAGE 70

STRAWBERRY-COCONUT LOAF CAKE

I've never been a fan of milk. Cheese, sure. Sour cream, sign me up! But milk? No thanks. I don't have a memory of ever drinking a glass of cow's milk, even as a kid. As a result, it's not a staple in my fridge. I am, however, a huge fan of coconut milk. It makes insanely good ice cream (see page 65), and it's my favorite liquid to use for French toast (with challah, of course—see page 161). This loaf cake is deliciously creamy and full of the good fat you need for baked goods.

CAKE

2⅓ cups + more for pan	all-purpose flour	280+ g
1 teaspoon	baking soda	6 g
1 teaspoon	baking powder	4 g
1 teaspoon	kosher salt	6 g
1 cup + 1 tablespoon	granulated sugar	213 g
1 cup	full-fat coconut milk (from well-shaken can)	220 g
½ cup	pilsner	113 g
¼ cup	vegetable oil	60 g
1 teaspoon	pure vanilla extract	5 g
1 cup	chopped strawberries	166 g

ICING

2 cups	powdered sugar	240 g
3 tablespoons	full-fat coconut milk (from well-shaken can)	42 g
1 teaspoon	pure vanilla extract	5 g
⅓ cup	sliced strawberries	55 g

TO MAKE THE CAKE: Preheat the oven to 325°F. Grease and flour an 8.5 × 4.5-inch loaf pan.

In a large bowl, whisk together the flour, baking soda, baking powder, salt, and sugar. Add the coconut milk, beer, oil, and vanilla and stir until just combined. Stir in the strawberries.

Pour the batter into the prepared pan and smooth the top. Bake until the top of the cake is golden brown and springs back when lightly touched, 65 to 75 minutes.

Remove the cake from the oven, allow it to cool for 1 hour in the pan, and then transfer it to a wire rack to cool completely.

TO MAKE THE ICING: Stir together the powdered sugar, coconut milk, and vanilla to make a thick paste.

When the cake is cool, top it with the icing. Sprinkle the iced cake with the sliced strawberries and serve.

GRILLED ROMAINE
WITH IPA-PICKLED STRAWBERRIES

—◈— SERVES 6 —◈—

This dish has two things that will surprise the hell out of your guests, prompting shocked-face questions: "You did what to the lettuce? You can do that? Wait, pickled what? Why?" But don't worry, once they've had a bite of the slightly smoky char of still-cold romaine with the briny sweetness of pickled strawberries, they'll be believers. Not just in the power of grilled or pickled produce, but in your ability to make an epic side dish. Be sure to start pickling the strawberries at least a day before you plan to serve the salad.

3	**romaine hearts**	
2 tablespoons + more for serving	**extra virgin olive oil**	30+ g
¼ cup	**shredded Parmigiano-Reggiano**	28 g
¼ cup	**chopped hazelnuts**	34 g
for serving	**IPA-Pickled Strawberries (recipe follows)**	
for serving	**balsamic vinegar**	

Prepare a charcoal grill for direct heat or heat a gas grill to medium-high.

Halve the romaine hearts lengthwise. Brush the cut sides with the olive oil. Place the romaine, cut side down, on the cooking grate. Grill until grill marks appear, about 3 minutes.

Transfer the grilled romaine to a serving platter. Top with the Parmigiano-Reggiano, hazelnuts, and some pickled strawberries. Drizzle the salad with olive oil and balsamic vinegar and serve.

⇒ IPA-PICKLED STRAWBERRIES ⇐

¾ cup	**red wine vinegar**	180 g
1 tablespoon	**kosher salt**	18 g
1 tablespoon	**granulated sugar**	13 g
½ cup	**imperial IPA**	113 g
1 cup	**quartered strawberries**	166 g

In a small saucepan, warm the vinegar over medium-high heat. Transfer the warm vinegar to an airtight container and add the salt and sugar. Stir until the salt and sugar dissolve. Stir in the beer.

Add the strawberries, cover, and refrigerate for at least 1 day and up to 2 weeks.

GRILLED
ROMAINE

PAGE 71

STROZZAPRETI
WITH LEMON CHARD AND SAISON CREAM SAUCE

I'm not sure why strozzapreti isn't as ubiquitous a noodle shape as fettuccine or macaroni—it's the best of both worlds. It's longer than macaroni, but far shorter than the slurp-needing length of fettuccine. It's got the tube-like crevasses of a macaroni noodle that help trap sauce, but with a longer, curved, elegant shape. Once you've sauced up these delightful little noodles, you'll be seeking them out over other shapes.

1 pound	**strozzapreti**	454 g
2 tablespoons	**unsalted butter**	28 g
1 tablespoon	**extra virgin olive oil**	15 g
1 small or ½ large	**shallot, chopped**	
4 cups	**chopped red chard**	60 g
2	**cloves garlic, minced**	
1 cup	**saison**	227 g
1 cup	**heavy cream**	240 g
3 tablespoons	**freshly squeezed lemon juice**	45 g
½ cup + more for topping	**shaved Parmigiano-Reggiano**	56+ g
½ teaspoon	**kosher salt**	3 g
½ teaspoon	**freshly ground black pepper**	2 g
pinch	**cayenne pepper**	

Bring a large pot of salted water to a boil over medium-high heat. Add the strozzapreti and cook until just before al dente, about 2 minutes before the time stated on the package directions (generally 8 to 10 minutes, depending on the brand). Reserve about ¼ cup of the pasta water, then drain the pasta.

Melt the butter and warm the olive oil in a large skillet over medium-high heat. Add the shallot and cook, stirring frequently, until just starting to brown, about 8 minutes. Stir in the chard and cook until softened, about 5 minutes. Stir in the garlic.

Reduce the heat to medium and stir in the beer, cream, and lemon juice. Add the Parmigiano-Reggiano a bit at a time, stirring to incorporate before adding more. Add the salt, black pepper, and cayenne. Taste and adjust the seasonings as needed.

Stir the pasta into the sauce and cook over medium heat until the sauce has thickened and the noodles have finished cooking, about 5 minutes. Add some of the reserved pasta water if the sauce becomes too thick.

Transfer the pasta to a serving bowl, sprinkle with additional Parmigiano-Reggiano, and serve.

BEER POLENTA
WITH CREAMY CHARD AND EGGS

Don't tell the other recipes, but this is one of my favorites in the book. It's OK—recipes aren't like children. You're allowed to have favorites, and this one might be first in line for any cheese-related inheritance I may have. The creamy, beer-spiked polenta is the perfect backdrop for the earthy, bright flavors of the chard, and, well, eggs with runny yolks just make everything better, don't they? Yolks really are nature's perfect sauce.

2½ cups	reduced-sodium vegetable broth	600 g
1 cup	pale ale	227 g
1 cup	dry polenta	140 g
½ cup	heavy cream	120 g
½ cup + more for garnish	shredded Parmigiano-Reggiano	56+ g
1½ teaspoons, divided	kosher salt	9 g
3 tablespoons	unsalted butter	42 g
3 cups	chopped red chard	100 g
2	cloves garlic, minced	
4	large eggs, poached (see Note on page 41)	

In a medium saucepan, combine the broth, beer, and polenta. Bring to a simmer over medium-high heat and cook, stirring occasionally, until the mixture has thickened and the polenta has softened, about 20 minutes.

Stir in the cream, Parmigiano-Reggiano, and 1 teaspoon (6 g) of the salt. Cook until the polenta has absorbed most of the liquid and is well combined with the cheese, about 5 minutes.

While the polenta cooks, melt the butter in a skillet over medium-high heat. Add the chard and cook, stirring occasionally, until softened, about 6 minutes. Stir in the garlic and remaining ½ teaspoon (3 g) of salt. Remove the pan from the heat.

Ladle the polenta into four serving bowls. Top each with some of the chard and a poached egg. Sprinkle with Parmigiano-Reggiano and serve warm.

SUMMER

/ ˈsə-mər /

NOUN: a period of maturing powers

NOUN: the warmest season of the year

Summer always seems to take its time, peeking out of the shadows of winter a few times in the spring to remind you that you want it, and that it'll be here soon. It'll give you a day of high 70s and sunshine before it ducks back, returning you to your previously scheduled rainy days. You remember how much you want to run barefoot in the grass, grill your dinner while wearing a tank top and those cut-off shorts you probably should have thrown out years ago. When it finally does grace us with its presence, it's more than just sunshine.

SUMMER PRODUCE

 denotes vegan recipe or easy vegan adaptations given

APPLES

I have strong feelings about apple varieties. Red Delicious, with their classic good looks, should only be visually enjoyed but never consumed (far too grainy and mealy!). Granny Smith is a go-to classic for baking, as it's tart and retains its shape even when cooked. Honeycrisp will always be one of my all-around favorites for baking, snacking, and overall visual appeal. In these recipes, stick to the variety I call for. The type of apple you use can make a world of difference, for better or for worse.

Beer-Sautéed Apple, Caramelized Onion, and Brie Sandwiches
page 85

Summer Ale Apple Pie with Beer Pie Dough
page 89

BELL PEPPERS

For something from the same family as the spicy habanero, bell peppers are surprisingly sweet. Producing no capsaicin (the stuff that makes a chile spicy), bell peppers give you a world of options. While you may think that the different-colored bell peppers are unique varieties, the green ones are actually unripened red guys, while the yellow and orange are phases in between. The red ones tend to have brighter, sweeter flavors than green peppers, which are often firmer and slightly tart.

Charred Pepper, Mozzarella, and ISA Romesco Sandwiches
page 91

Grilled Red Pepper Sauce
page 95

BLUEBERRIES

Last year the neighbor's dog, Quigley—a fat, old-man pug—got loose. We found him in a nearby blueberry bush, sitting content and happy. He'd cleaned off all the fruit from the bottom half of the bush and was making no apologies for it. Really, can you blame him? When I come into ownership of a large stash of blueberries, I usually sort out my loot into two piles: the firm ones just get popped into my mouth and eaten like candy, and the softer ones get saved for baking or frozen for later. When buying these beauties, look for firm, bright berries without any signs of wrinkling or wilting.

Blueberry-Basil Hefeweizen Custard
page 96

Blueberry-Lavender Summer Ale Clafoutis
page 99

CHERRIES

Over the years, I've tried to sneak cherries into almost every dish. Chocolate cake? Check. Pie? Obviously. Pizza? Yep. Salad? The best. I've even pickled them, roasted them, and sautéed them. I freeze them for the months I can't find them, and I make batches of cocktail cherries to enjoy throughout the year in drinks and on desserts. I'm partial to Bing cherries, but Lapins and Lambert cherries are excellent runners-up. As long as you find a cherry with a dark red exterior and a sweet flavor, you're all set. Want to know the secret for finding the freshest cherries? Look for a stem that is intact and green; they turn brown and fall off as they age.

Gose Cocktail Cherries 🍃
page 101

Bing Cherry and Hefeweizen Farro Salad with Mirin-Lime Dressing 🍃
page 102

CUCUMBERS

Two types of cucumbers dominate my kitchen: English and Kirby. English are your standard, easy to find, long cucumbers with a thick skin and a mild flavor. Also known as European, seedless, or hothouse cucumbers, they can often be found individually shrink-wrapped in plastic. These are perfect for salads and just slicing and eating. Kirbys are for pickling. They're also for hollowing out and serving dip in, but we'll get to that in a few pages. If you can't find Kirbys, Persian cucumbers make an excellent stand-in. Make sure the cucumbers you choose are firm; they soften as they age.

Cucumber Cups with Avocado and White Ale Bean Purée 🍃
page 105

Spicy Beer Pickles 🍃
page 106

JALAPEÑOS

Eating jalapeños is like online dating: you never really know what you're in for. You could find one on the mild side with a bold jalapeño-y flavor that's fun and interesting. You could also get a face-meltingly hot little jerk who just wants to hurt you. To control the heat, you've got to gut them (just talking about the peppers, not the bad dates). Fiery capsaicin is concentrated in the membranes and coats the seeds of chilies. Removing both will help level the playing field while still retaining the flavor of the pepper that we love so much.

Jalapeño-Kölsch Cornbread
page 109

Cilantro, Beer, and Cream Cheese Crostini with Cherry Salsa and ISA-Candied Jalapeños
page 110

PEACHES

I tend to favor yellow peaches over white. White peaches are usually more expensive anyhow, and flavor isn't the reason. It's because white peaches bruise more easily than their golden counterparts and thus fewer make it to market. While both are lovely and fairly interchangeable when it comes to baking, I find the flavor of yellow peaches bolder, more balanced, and more classically peachy. It's best to store peaches at room temperature, stem side down.

Flatbreads with Beer-Pickled Peaches, Jalapeño, and Mozzarella
page 114

Grilled Peaches with ISA-Mint Chimichurri 🍃
page 116

TOMATILLOS

Although the name of these little guys means "little tomato" in Spanish and, husked, they look like little tomatoes, they're not, in any way, little tomatoes. Even head to head with green tomatoes, tomatillos are brighter, more acidic, and more vegetal. Use them for salsa verde, pozole, or a pickled sandwich topping—they are so versatile! Most supermarkets carry them, and you are nearly guaranteed to find them at a market specializing in Mexican ingredients.

TOMATOES

There is nothing more satisfying for the novice gardener than the first ripe tomato of the season. From out of nowhere, the plant goes from flowering to full of little green gems. Once the first brave tomato decides to yellow in late spring, the rest take the hint and jump on the red-ripening bandwagon. It's thrilling to watch, and even more satisfying to sit down to a dinner of your garden bounty. If you're at all interested in trying your hand at growing food, I heartily suggest starting with a simple tomato plant. If it's not in the cards for you right now, stop in at your local farmers markets for the best finds. Look for heirloom varieties, and favor those that are heavy for their size.

WATERMELON

For something so tasty, this garden candy packs a healthy punch, with far more lycopene than tomatoes and vitamins such as A, B6, C, and thiamin. I'm sold! Don't tell the watermelon, but I'd eat it even if it were bad for me. At the market, choose one that is heavy for its size and has a creamy yellow (not white) spot on it. Yep, you want a big, ugly yellow spot on your melon. That means it sat in the real-life sun to ripen, which makes it sweeter and juicier. If the spot doesn't exist, it was picked too soon and didn't ripen in the sun.

SUMMER BEERS

Summer is more than a season, it's a lifestyle. It's lazy days on the river, evening parties on the patio, beach vacations, and trips to the lake. It's also a cooler full of beer. Summer beer takes on a life of its own: it's hoppier, it's more carbonated, and (thankfully) it's even lower in ABV than the beers of spring. The lower alcohol levels aren't because we suddenly can't hold our booze once the weather heats up—they're because we tend to spend more time drinking, and the low ABV beer helps us avoid becoming cautionary tales.

SUMMER ALE. Although "summer ale" isn't a proper category and has no official definition, that doesn't stop breweries from releasing thousands of these enigmatic ales every year. They will, however, almost always be a good choice for a hot day. Most are light bodied, often a touch fruity, a bit hoppy with a lower malt character, and nicely carbonated.

KÖLSCH. If you haven't enjoyed a crisp kölsch on a hot day, you need to reevaluate your pastime activities. Clean, mild, light, and crisp, these are beers that you can drink all day long, and with lower ABV, it's a good choice when deciding to do so. It's the perfect beer to enjoy at a backyard cookout, as it readily makes friends with grilled foods and high heat.

SESSION IPA OR ISA. These are beers that do you a big favor. They're big on hops and flavor but generally below 5 percent ABV, so you can have quite a few and still stay on your feet. Try that with a 10 percent triple IPA and you'll understand what I mean. Most ISAs are full of hop flavor, lower in malt character (although malt will still be present), and nicely carbonated, much like typical IPAs. The big difference is found in that low ABV.

GOSE. Sure, lots of sour beers make an appearance this time of year, but the gose is summer in a can. Bright, fruity, tangy, and with a hint of salt, it's the perfect beer to pair with a day at the beach, a float down the river, or a backyard cookout.

WHEAT BEER AND FRUITED WHEAT. Wheat beers, like white ales, witbiers, and hefeweizens, just go down easy in the summer heat. The yeast is often a dominant flavor, and you can expect notes of fruit, citrus, banana, clove, and bread. Brewers like to spike wheat beer with fruit or fruit juice when summer rolls around, giving them a taste of the season. Also look for a radler or a shandy (part beer and part lemonade, orange juice, or grapefruit juice). These may not be the top choices for all beer drinkers, but they can be perfect for your lightweight of a date. Hefeweizen is a wheat beer with a mild sweetness and present but approachable flavors, plus a nice carbonation that can cut through anything fatty or greasy you want to serve it with. Its big flavors can stand up to the heat of a spicy pepper but also work well with a sweeter dish.

BEER-SAUTÉED APPLE, CARAMELIZED ONION, AND BRIE SANDWICHES

Yeah, I know, grilled cheese is supposed to be a quick-and-dirty way to feed your face. It's hangover food, it's don't-wanna-grocery-shop food, it's not cookbook food. Unless, of course, you add creamy brie and beer-caramelized onions. If it makes you feel better, you can totally grill it in a panini press to make it even fancier.

2 tablespoons	**extra virgin olive oil**	30 g
1	**sweet white onion, sliced**	
1 tablespoon, packed	**golden brown sugar**	14 g
1½ cups, divided	**hefeweizen**	340 g
4 tablespoons, divided, + more for griddle	**unsalted butter**	56+ g
1	**large Granny Smith apple, cored and cut into ⅛-inch slices**	
1 teaspoon	**kosher salt**	6 g
1 loaf	**brioche**	
8 ounces	**brie, thinly sliced**	227 g

Heat the oil in a large sauté pan over medium heat. Don't let the oil get too hot, or the onion will burn before it caramelizes. Add the onion and cook, stirring occasionally, until it softens, about 5 minutes.

Stir in the brown sugar and continue cooking the onion until it has darkened and is starting to caramelize, about 20 minutes. Add 1 cup (227 g) of the beer, scraping the bottom of the pan to deglaze it. Cook until the beer is mostly gone and the onion is dark brown, about 20 minutes. Remove the pan from the heat and set aside.

Melt 2 tablespoons (28 g) of the butter in a skillet over medium-high heat. Add the apple slices and salt. Cook, stirring, until the apples start to soften, about 10 minutes. Add the remaining ½ cup (113 g) of beer. Cook until the apples are soft and the beer is mostly gone, about 10 minutes.

Preheat the oven to 400°F. Heat a griddle or large skillet over medium-high heat. Set a wire rack in a rimmed baking sheet.

Cut 12 (½-inch) slices from the brioche. Use the remaining 2 tablespoons (28 g) of butter to spread one side of each slice of brioche. Place one slice, buttered side down, on the griddle. Top it with some of the brie, caramelized onion, and apple slices, then additional brie, and cover with another slice of brioche, buttered side up. Cook until the bottom has browned, flip the sandwich, and cook until the other side has browned. Transfer the sandwich to the wire rack. Repeat this process with the remaining ingredients.

Transfer the baking sheet with the wire rack of sandwiches to the oven and bake until the cheese has melted, about 6 minutes. Serve immediately.

BEER-SAUTÉED APPLE,
CARAMELIZED ONION,
AND BRIE SANDWICHES

PAGE 85

SUMMER ALE APPLE PIE
WITH BEER PIE DOUGH

Sure, apples take center stage in fall when the collective baking community renews an obsession with these crisp, juicy beauties, but they actually come into season in the late summer—just in time for the last gasps of summer cookouts and the summer ales that are about to become scarce. It's the perfect way to gracefully bow out of summer and welcome in the autumn weather.

DOUGH

2½ cups, divided	all-purpose flour	300 g
1 teaspoon	kosher salt	6 g
2 tablespoons	granulated sugar	26 g
1½ sticks	unsalted butter, chilled and cubed	171 g
½ cup	vegetable shortening	205 g
⅓ cup	ice-cold summer ale	74 g

FILLING

2–3	large Honeycrisp apples, peeled, cored, and sliced	
2–3	large Granny Smith apples, peeled, cored, and sliced	
½ cup, packed	golden brown sugar	110 g
¼ cup	all-purpose flour	30 g
1 teaspoon	ground cinnamon	3 g
¼ teaspoon	ground nutmeg	1 g
1 tablespoon	freshly squeezed lemon juice	15 g
1 tablespoon	summer ale	14 g
2 tablespoons	unsweetened applesauce	32 g

ASSEMBLY

for dusting	all-purpose flour	
2 tablespoons	unsalted butter, melted	28 g
½ cup	granulated sugar	100 g
8 ounces	mascarpone	227 g
1 cup	powdered sugar	120 g
1 teaspoon	pure vanilla extract	5 g
2 tablespoons	summer ale	28 g

TO MAKE THE DOUGH: Combine 1½ cups (180 g) of the flour, the salt, and the sugar in the bowl of a food processor and pulse to combine. Add the cold butter and shortening and process until well combined and the dough gathers around the blade. Add the remaining 1 cup (120 g) of flour and pulse six to eight times, until all the flour has been moistened.

Transfer the dough to a bowl. Using a rubber spatula, stir in the beer until it is completely incorporated into the dough (don't add the beer in the food processor or your dough will turn into a cracker once baked). The dough should be very soft.

Lay two long sheets of plastic wrap on a work surface. Divide the dough in half, and place one half in the middle of each sheet. Form each portion of the dough into a disk. Wrap each disk tightly in the plastic and transfer to the refrigerator to chill until firm, about 1 hour.

RECIPE CONTINUES ☞

SUMMER ALE APPLE PIE WITH
BEER PIE DOUGH

CONTINUED

TO MAKE THE FILLING: Preheat the oven to 350°F.

Combine the Honeycrisp and Granny Smith apples in a large bowl. Sprinkle them with the brown sugar, flour, cinnamon, nutmeg, lemon juice, beer, and applesauce. Toss the apples until coated.

TO ASSEMBLE: Lightly flour a clean, dry work surface. Roll out one of the dough disks to a 12-inch circle. Line a 9-inch pie pan with the dough and trim off the excess. Pour the filling into the pie pan.

Roll out the remaining dough to a 10-inch circle. With a 1-inch cookie cutter (I like the star shape, but a circle or any other shape will work), punch out shapes and lay them over the filling. Brush the dough shapes with the melted butter and sprinkle with the granulated sugar.

Place the pie in the freezer for 10 minutes. Transfer the pie to the oven and bake for 40 minutes or until the top is golden brown. Allow the pie to cool for at least 1 hour before cutting.

When ready to serve, in a small bowl, whisk together the mascarpone, powdered sugar, vanilla, and beer until well combined. Top the pie with the cream, slice, and serve.

CHARRED PEPPER, MOZZARELLA, AND ISA ROMESCO SANDWICHES

Romesco sauce is one of my favorite ways to enjoy red bell peppers. Originally developed by fishermen in a small coastal village in Spain, the mix of garlic, nuts, and spices gives the perfect balance of beautiful flavors. It's so versatile and easy to scoop out of the bowl with just about anything from pita bread to your car keys. In this case, it's a delightful sandwich spread that turns out to be the star of the dish.

1	large yellow bell pepper, stemmed, halved, and seeded	
1	large poblano pepper, stemmed, halved, and seeded	
4	ciabatta rolls	
	ISA Romesco (recipe follows)	
8 ounces	fresh mozzarella, sliced	227 g
1 cup	baby arugula	25 g

Position an oven rack 3 inches from the broiler. Preheat the broiler.

Place the peppers, cut side down, on a rimmed baking sheet. Broil until the skin has wrinkled and blackened, about 8 minutes. Transfer the peppers to a large bowl and cover with aluminum foil or plastic wrap. Allow the peppers to steam for 10 minutes, until softened and cooled slightly. Rub to remove and discard the peppers' blackened skin, then thinly slice the peppers.

Split the ciabatta rolls. Spread each cut side with romesco. Transfer them, face up, to a rimmed baking sheet. Top each half with some pepper slices and mozzarella.

Broil the rolls until the mozzarella starts to melt, about 8 minutes. Top half of the rolls with arugula, then sandwich the remaining halves of the ciabatta together. Serve warm.

RECIPE CONTINUES ☞

CHARRED PEPPER, MOZZARELLA, AND ISA ROMESCO SANDWICHES

CONTINUED

≫ ISA ROMESCO ≪

1	large red bell pepper, stemmed, halved, and seeded	
⅔ cup	sliced almonds	79 g
1	clove garlic, peeled and lightly smashed	
1 (6-ounce) can	tomato paste	170 g
2 tablespoons	chopped fresh flat-leaf parsley leaves	2 g
3 tablespoons	session IPA or ISA	43 g
1 teaspoon	red pepper flakes	2 g
½ teaspoon	smoked paprika	1 g
½ teaspoon	sea salt	3 g
½ teaspoon	freshly ground black pepper	2 g
¼ cup	extra virgin olive oil	60 g

Position an oven rack 3 inches from the broiler. Preheat the broiler.

Place the pepper, cut side down, on a rimmed baking sheet. Broil until the skin has wrinkled and blackened, about 8 minutes. Transfer the pepper to a large bowl and cover with aluminum foil or plastic wrap. Allow the pepper to steam for 10 minutes, until softened and cooled slightly. Rub to remove and discard the pepper's blackened skin.

Toast the almonds in a skillet over medium-high heat, sliding the pan back and forth across the burner and tossing the almonds until they are lightly toasted, about 3 minutes. Keep a close eye, as they burn quickly.

Combine the toasted almonds, roasted red pepper, garlic, tomato paste, parsley, beer, red pepper flakes, paprika, salt, and black pepper in the bowl of a food processor. Process for about 1 minute; then, with the machine running, slowly add the olive oil through the feed tube until well combined.

Use right away or store in an airtight container in the refrigerator for up to 1 week.

GRILLED RED PEPPER SAUCE

MAKES 1½ CUPS

Have you ever grilled garlic? Stop right now, put this book down, and fire up your grill. Glorious grilled garlic pairs perfectly with the sweet meat of a perfectly grilled red pepper, which sends this sauce over the top. What can you do with this sauce? What can't you do! Pizza sauce: check. Sandwich spread: check. Pasta topping: double check. Eating it with a spoon all alone in your kitchen: umm, check.

2	**red bell peppers**	
1	**white onion, quartered**	
6	**large cloves garlic, peeled**	
⅓ cup + more for grill	**extra virgin olive oil**	80+ g
½ cup	**kölsch**	113 g
2 teaspoons	**chopped fresh oregano leaves**	6 g
1 teaspoon	**chopped fresh basil leaves**	0.5 g
1 teaspoon	**kosher salt**	6 g
½ teaspoon	**red pepper flakes**	1.5 g
1 (6-ounce) can	**tomato paste**	170 g

Prepare a charcoal grill for direct heat or heat a gas grill to medium-high.

Brush the bell peppers, onion, and garlic with a bit of olive oil. Transfer them to the grill. If the garlic is too small to sit on the grate, place a small square of aluminum foil on the grate and set the garlic on top.

Grill the vegetables, turning occasionally, until the garlic and onion are soft and the skin of the bell peppers is completely blackened, 3 to 5 minutes per side. Remove the vegetables from the grill as they finish cooking. The bell peppers will take the longest.

Transfer the bell peppers to a large bowl and cover with aluminum foil or plastic wrap. Allow the peppers to steam for 10 minutes, until softened and cooled slightly. Rub to remove and discard the peppers' blackened skin. Transfer the onion and garlic to the bowl of a food processor. Add the bell peppers, olive oil, beer, oregano, basil, salt, red pepper flakes, and tomato paste.

Process until smooth. Use immediately or store in an airtight container in the refrigerator for up to 7 days.

BLUEBERRY-BASIL
HEFEWEIZEN CUSTARD

SERVES 6

You can, of course, serve this custard in cute little glass dishes topped with whipped cream and fresh berries, but there is so much more it can be used for. I've poured it into a pie crust, piped it into doughnuts, dolloped it on top of pancakes—it really has so many uses. Feel free to add whipped cream or even a little shortbread cookie. This is a recipe you can customize to your own preferences.

1 cup	heavy cream	240 g
1 cup	whole milk	240 g
½ cup	hefeweizen	113 g
1	large egg	
3	large egg yolks	
⅓ cup	granulated sugar	66 g
1 teaspoon	kosher salt	6 g
2 tablespoons	cornstarch	26 g
1 teaspoon	pure vanilla extract	5 g
2 teaspoons	minced fresh basil leaves	1 g
⅔ cup, divided	blueberries	80 g

Combine the cream, milk, and beer in a saucepan and heat over medium heat, stirring occasionally, for about 5 minutes, until it is just warmed and bubbles start to form around the edges. Remove the pan from the heat.

In a medium bowl, whisk together the egg, yolks, sugar, salt, cornstarch, and vanilla. While whisking, pour the warm milk mixture into the egg mixture, a little at a time, until it is completely incorporated.

Return the egg mixture to the saucepan, along with the basil and ⅓ cup (40 g) of the blueberries. Cook the egg mixture over medium heat, whisking continuously, until it has thickened, about 6 minutes.

Pour the custard into serving bowls and refrigerate until completely chilled, about 2 hours. Serve topped with the remaining ⅓ cup (40 g) blueberries.

BLUEBERRY-LAVENDER
SUMMER ALE CLAFOUTIS

Clafoutis (pronounced klah-FOO-tee) is the simple French baking recipe that you didn't know you needed. It's gorgeous, delicious, simple to prepare, and perfect for any type of summer fruit that you find yourself inundated with. For something with so few steps, this is an epically beautiful way to serve breakfast, dessert, or an afternoon snack. It's part pancake, part muffin, and all delicious.

½ cup	heavy cream	120 g
½ cup	summer ale	113 g
3	large eggs	
½ cup	granulated sugar	100 g
1 teaspoon	minced fresh English lavender leaves	1 g
1 teaspoon	pure vanilla extract	5 g
½ teaspoon	kosher salt	3 g
2 tablespoons	unsalted butter, melted	28 g
½ cup	all-purpose flour	60 g
⅓ cup	blueberries	40 g
for serving	powdered sugar	

Preheat the oven to 350°F.

In a mixing bowl, whisk together the cream, beer, eggs, sugar, lavender, vanilla, salt, and melted butter. Whisk in the flour.

Pour the batter into a 9-inch cast iron skillet. Scatter the blueberries over the top. Bake until the top is light golden brown, about 35 minutes.

Remove the skillet from the oven, sprinkle the clafoutis with powdered sugar, and serve warm.

GOSE COCKTAIL CHERRIES

Even if your cocktails don't include beer, they should include beer-soaked cocktail cherries. They're so simple to make, and they are the perfect addition to a hostess gift basket for someone whose house you'd like to be reinvited to. You'll need to start this recipe a couple of days before you intend to serve them.

1 cup	**gose**	227 g
½ cup	**spiced rum**	113 g
1 cup, packed	**golden brown sugar**	220 g
8 ounces	**dark cherries, pitted**	227 g

Combine the beer, rum, and brown sugar in a saucepan and simmer over medium-high heat until the sugar has dissolved, about 3 minutes.

Put the cherries in an airtight container. Pour the beer mixture over the cherries. Allow the cherries to sit at room temperature for 1 hour. Cover and refrigerate for at least 2 days before serving. Store the cherries in the refrigerator for up to 2 weeks.

BING CHERRY AND HEFEWEIZEN
FARRO SALAD
WITH MIRIN-LIME DRESSING

If there is a fruit I would wait outside the market for with my face pressed against the glass until they ripen and are ready to eat, it would be cherries. These little beauties, with their gemstone good looks and the mischievous way they make you look like you've murdered someone when you try to pit them, are the perfect way to turn an ordinary salad into something everyone will remember. Just don't forget the apron so you can leave the bloodlike spatter at home. Farro is my favorite ancient grain and replaces rice in my kitchen on most occasions. I love the slightly nutty flavor, the chewiness, and the fact that it's packed with protein.

SALAD

1 cup	hefeweizen	227 g
1½ cups	water	354 g
1 cup	pearled farro	200 g
½ teaspoon	kosher salt	3 g
1 cup	pitted, quartered Bing cherries	170 g
1 cup	baby arugula	25 g
¼ cup	crumbled goat cheese (optional)	38 g

DRESSING

1 tablespoon	minced fresh basil leaves	1 g
3 tablespoons	mirin	36 g
2 tablespoons	extra virgin olive oil	30 g
1 tablespoon	red wine vinegar	15 g
1 teaspoon	freshly squeezed lime juice	11 g
pinch	sea salt	

TO MAKE THE SALAD: Combine the beer and water in a small saucepan and bring to a boil over high heat. Stir in the farro and salt and reduce the heat to medium-low. Cover and simmer for 30 minutes or until the farro is soft and chewy.

Drain the farro and transfer it to a serving bowl. Set the farro aside to cool to room temperature. Add the cherries, arugula, and goat cheese to the cooled farro, tossing to combine.

TO MAKE THE DRESSING: In a small bowl, whisk together the basil, mirin, olive oil, vinegar, lime juice, and salt. Add the dressing as desired to the salad. Serve immediately.

CUCUMBER CUPS
WITH AVOCADO AND WHITE ALE BEAN PURÉE

The first time I made a cup out of cucumber was a revelation. Just a cut and a flip of the melon baller and bam! You're all set. It's a cute little dip receptacle that you can fill with anything. In this case, I've chosen a purée that's packed with the buttery texture of avocado and the zippy flavor of hummus. The warm, creamy purée is perfect against the cool snap of the cucumber.

1 (15-ounce) can	**great Northern beans, rinsed and drained**	425 g
¼ cup	**tahini**	60 g
¼ cup	**white ale**	57 g
1	**large avocado, peeled and pitted**	
1½ teaspoons	**garlic powder**	8 g
1 teaspoon	**kosher salt**	6 g
½ teaspoon	**freshly ground black pepper**	3 g
½ teaspoon	**sweet paprika**	3 g
5	**medium Kirby or Persian cucumbers**	
1 tablespoon	**chopped fresh chives**	1 g

Combine the beans, tahini, beer, avocado, garlic powder, salt, pepper, and paprika in a blender. Blend until the mixture is smooth.

Cut the cucumbers crosswise into 1½-inch sections. Using a melon baller or a paring knife, scoop out and discard the center of each cucumber section, leaving the walls and bottom intact to create a cup.

Fill the cucumber cups with the bean purée. Sprinkle the tops with chives. Serve immediately.

SPICY BEER PICKLES

When summer rolls around and cucumbers start to spill out of the garden in abundance, this recipe is your response. Everyone wants a pickle on their plate, especially when that pickle took a long soak in a hoppy beer. Add the kick of some spice and it's the perfect companion at your summer cookout.

1½ cups	**session IPA**	340 g
1 cup	**apple cider vinegar**	240 g
¼ cup	**granulated sugar**	50 g
2 tablespoons	**kosher salt**	36 g
1 tablespoon	**whole black peppercorns**	12 g
2 teaspoons	**red pepper flakes**	4 g
2–3	**medium Kirby or Persian cucumbers, sliced (see Note)**	
5	**sprigs fresh dill**	

In a small saucepan, combine the beer, vinegar, sugar, salt, peppercorns, and red pepper flakes. While stirring, bring to a simmer over medium-high heat and cook just until the sugar and salt dissolve, about 3 minutes. Remove the brine from the heat and let it cool to room temperature.

Pack the cucumbers into an airtight container. Add the dill. Pour the cooled brine over the cucumbers, making sure everything is submerged.

Cover and refrigerate for at least 24 hours before serving. Store in the refrigerator as is for up to 1 week, or can properly for shelf storage.

NOTE

Cucumbers can be sliced into coins or cut into spears, whichever you prefer.

JALAPEÑO-KÖLSCH CORNBREAD

SERVES 8

Cornbread is the perfect side dish. It's got some vegetables to satisfy that nagging urge. It's also bread, which is always welcome, and it can double as a bun when you're in a pinch and want to make yourself an impromptu sandwich. Leftover grilled corn works perfect here!

1	ear yellow corn, husk and silk removed	
1 tablespoon	extra virgin olive oil	15 g
1¼ cups	cornmeal	188 g
¾ cup	all-purpose flour	90 g
2	jalapeños, seeded and chopped	
⅓ cup, packed	golden brown sugar	73 g
1½ teaspoons	baking soda	9 g
1½ teaspoons	baking powder	6 g
1 teaspoon	kosher salt	6 g
1 stick	unsalted butter, melted	114 g
¾ cup	kölsch	170 g
2	large eggs, lightly beaten	
¼ cup	vegetable oil	60 g
2 tablespoons	unsalted butter	28 g

Prepare a charcoal grill for direct heat or heat a gas grill to medium-high. Preheat the oven to 400°F.

Brush the corn all over with the olive oil. Grill the corn, turning occasionally, until grill marks appear on all sides.

Cut the kernels from the cob and transfer them to a large bowl. Add the cornmeal, flour, jalapeños, brown sugar, baking soda, baking powder, and salt and stir to combine.

Make a well in the center of the corn mixture. Add the melted butter, beer, eggs, and vegetable oil to the center of the well and stir until the batter is just combined.

Put the butter in a 9-inch cast iron skillet and transfer to the oven. Remove the skillet when the butter is melted and the skillet is hot, about 2 minutes.

Swirl the pan to coat it evenly with the melted butter. Add the batter and smooth the top. Bake for 16 to 18 minutes, until the cornbread is lightly browned and the top springs back when touched.

Remove the skillet from the oven and allow the cornbread to cool slightly before slicing and serving.

CILANTRO, BEER, AND CREAM CHEESE CROSTINI
WITH CHERRY SALSA AND ISA-CANDIED JALAPEÑOS

SERVES 6

Candied jalapeños make a delightful pairing with cherry salsa. These two summer favorites will duke it out for star of the dish. Each will have a shining moment, but in the end, you'll realize that candied jalapeños are so spectacular and rare that they'll take the heavyweight belt every time.

1	baguette, sliced	
3 tablespoons	extra virgin olive oil	45 g
8 ounces	cream cheese	227 g
¼ cup	chopped fresh cilantro leaves	6 g
3 tablespoons	ISA	43 g
1 cup	pitted, chopped dark cherries	170 g
1	medium shallot, chopped	
pinch	kosher salt	
2 tablespoons	sherry vinegar	30 g
	ISA-Candied Jalapeños (recipe follows)	

Preheat the broiler.

Spread out the baguette slices on a rimmed baking sheet and brush them with the olive oil. Broil the bread slices until they are nicely toasted, about 3 minutes. Remove the baking sheet from the oven.

Put the cream cheese and cilantro in a bowl. Using a hand mixer set on high speed, whip the mixture, slowly adding the beer, a splash at a time, until all is incorporated.

In another bowl, combine the cherries, shallot, salt, and vinegar, tossing until the cherries are well coated.

Spread the cream cheese mixture on the toasted bread slices. Top each with some cherry salsa and then a few slices of candied jalapeños. Serve immediately.

⇛ ISA-CANDIED JALAPEÑOS ⇚

1 cup	session IPA	127 g
½ cup	apple cider vinegar	120 g
2 cups, packed	golden brown sugar	440 g
1 teaspoon	garlic powder	3 g
½ teaspoon	freshly ground black pepper	2 g
¼ teaspoon	ground allspice	0.25 g
15–18 large	jalapeños, cut crosswise into ¼-inch rings	

Combine the beer, vinegar, brown sugar, garlic powder, black pepper, and allspice in a saucepan and bring to a boil over medium-high heat. Boil the beer mixture for 6 minutes.

Stir in the jalapeños, remove the pan from the heat, and set it aside for 10 minutes. Drain the jalapeño rings, transfer them to a silicone baking mat or parchment paper, and allow to cool. Use right away or store in an airtight container in the fridge for up to 1 week.

FLATBREADS

PAGE 114

FLATBREADS
WITH BEER-PICKLED PEACHES, JALAPEÑO, AND MOZZARELLA

MAKES 8 FLATBREADS

This isn't the first time I've pickled peaches for a recipe, and it won't be the last. The tangy brine brings out a new layer of sweetness that goes well with so many dishes. And everyone loves flatbreads—they're like mini pizzas! Be sure to start pickling the peaches at least a day before you plan to make the flatbreads.

2¼ cups + more for dusting	bread flour	300+ g
1 (2¼-teaspoon) packet	fast-rising instant yeast	7 g
½ teaspoon	garlic powder	2 g
¾ cup	summer ale	170 g
5 tablespoons, divided	extra virgin olive oil	75 g
1 teaspoon, divided	kosher salt	6 g
8 ounces	fresh mozzarella, cut into ¼-inch slices	227 g
	Beer-Pickled Peaches (recipe follows)	
1	jalapeño, thinly sliced	
2 tablespoons	minced fresh cilantro leaves	2 g

In the bowl of a stand mixer fitted with the dough hook attachment, mix the flour, yeast, and garlic powder on medium speed until combined.

Put the beer in a microwave-safe bowl. Microwave on high for 20 seconds. Test the beer's temperature with an instant-read thermometer and repeat this process until it registers between 120°F and 125°F or reaches the temperature specified on the package of yeast.

Add the beer to the flour mixture and mix on medium speed until most of the flour has been moistened. With the mixer running, add 3 tablespoons (45 g) of the olive oil and ½ teaspoon (3 g) of the salt. Increase the speed to high and beat the dough until it is smooth and elastic, about 8 minutes.

Lightly grease a large bowl. Transfer the dough to the bowl and cover it tightly with plastic wrap. Allow the dough to sit in a warm place until it has doubled in size, 45 to 60 minutes.

Prepare a charcoal grill for direct heat or heat a gas grill to medium-high.

Lightly flour a clean, dry work surface. Turn out the dough and knead it several times, until the dough starts to stiffen a bit. Cut the dough into 8 equal-size pieces. Working with one piece of dough at a time, form them into 6-inch circles.

Use some of the remaining 2 tablespoons (30 g) of olive oil to brush one side of each dough circle. Place the circles, oiled side down, on the cooking grate. Brush the tops with oil. Grill until grill marks appear on the bottom, about 4 minutes, then flip the dough. Immediately top with the cheese, pickled peaches, and jalapeño. Close the lid and grill until the dough is cooked through and the cheese has melted, about 5 minutes.

Transfer the flatbreads to a serving platter. Sprinkle them with the cilantro, season with the remaining ½ teaspoon (3 g) salt, and serve immediately.

⇉ BEER-PICKLED PEACHES ⇇

¼ cup	very hot water	57 g
2 tablespoons	kosher salt	36 g
1 tablespoon	granulated sugar	13 g
¾ cup	apple cider vinegar	180 g
½ cup	summer ale	113 g
2	large peaches, pitted and thinly sliced	

In an airtight container, combine the hot water, salt, and sugar and stir until the salt and sugar are dissolved. Stir in the vinegar and beer. Add the peaches, cover, and refrigerate for at least 1 day and up to 1 week.

GRILLED PEACHES
WITH ISA-MINT CHIMICHURRI

I grill peaches all summer. Want a dessert? I'll grill a peach and add some vanilla ice cream and a little caramel sauce! How about an appetizer? Grilled peaches are perfect with chimichurri! Serve this as a side dish next to salad or a nice grilled sandwich, or just line them up on a serving platter as a simple but satisfying appetizer.

2	large, ripe but firm yellow peaches, pitted and sliced	
2 tablespoons	extra virgin olive oil	30 g
for serving	ISA-Mint Chimichurri (recipe follows)	

Prepare a charcoal grill for direct heat or heat a gas grill to medium-high.

Brush the peach slices with the olive oil and place them on the cooking grate. Grill the peaches until grill marks appear, about 3 minutes. Flip them and grill the other side until grill marks appear and the peach slices are slightly softened, about 4 minutes.

Transfer the grilled peach slices to a serving dish. Drizzle them with the chimichurri as desired. Serve immediately.

⇗ ISA-MINT CHIMICHURRI ⇖

2	cloves garlic, minced	
1	large shallot, minced	
¼ cup, packed	chopped fresh spearmint leaves	6 g
½ cup, packed	chopped fresh flat-leaf parsley leaves	8 g
3 tablespoons	extra virgin olive oil	45 g
3 tablespoons	ISA	43 g
1 tablespoon	red wine vinegar	15 g
½ teaspoon	kosher salt	3 g
¼ teaspoon	red pepper flakes	0.5 g

Combine all the ingredients in a small bowl, stirring to combine. Use right away or store in an airtight container in the refrigerator for up to 1 week.

FRIED BEER–BATTERED TOMATILLO AND MOZZARELLA SLIDERS

MAKES 8 SLIDERS

When I visited Atlanta, Georgia, for the first time, I tried fried green anything. Served to me on an old, floral-patterned china plate, my first fried green tomato was a thing of beauty. Back on the West Coast I discovered that green tomatoes were nearly impossible to find. Tomatillos, however, were in abundance and made an excellent stand-in. Look for the biggest ones you can find—they make the best candidates for batter-dipping and deep-frying.

4	large tomatillos, husked and cut crosswise into ½-inch slices	
1 teaspoon	kosher salt	6 g
1 cup	kölsch	227 g
½ cup	buttermilk	105 g
½ cup	cornmeal	95 g
½ cup	all-purpose flour	60 g
1 tablespoon, packed	golden brown sugar	14 g
2 teaspoons	Creole seasoning	6 g
for frying	canola, safflower, or peanut oil	
8	slider buns	
1 cup	sour cream	240 g
1 tablespoon	Sriracha	
6 ounces	fresh mozzarella, sliced	
3	fresh basil leaves, cut into ribbons	

Season the tomatillo slices with the salt.

In a medium bowl, stir together the beer and buttermilk. Add the tomatillo slices, making sure they are submerged. Allow them to sit for 10 minutes while you prep the dredge.

In another medium bowl, stir together the cornmeal, flour, sugar, and Creole seasoning.

Pour about 2 inches of oil into a sauté pan or deep skillet and heat it over medium-high heat. Dip the handle of a wooden spoon into the oil to test the temperature. The oil is ready when bubbles begin to appear around the tip of the handle (approximately 350°F). Reduce the heat if the oil begins to smoke or darken.

One at a time, remove a slice of tomatillo from the liquid, dredge it in the flour mixture, dunk it again in the liquid, and then dredge it one more time in the flour mixture. Gently place the breaded slices in the hot oil. Cook on both sides until golden brown, about 2 minutes per side, then transfer to a paper towel–lined plate to drain. Cook two or three at a time, taking care not to crowd the pan.

Split the slider buns. Stir together the sour cream and Sriracha. Spread the insides of the buns with the sour cream mixture.

Place one or two tomatillo slices on each bun. Add a slice of mozzarella and a sprinkle of basil to each. Serve.

ROASTED TOMATILLO, MINT, AND SUMMER ALE POZOLE

SERVES 6

Sure, pozole is soup, which may lead you to think of colder seasons, but it's really the perfect summer meal. Especially since this gorgeous soup originated in the warm climate of Mexico, it's perfect for a hot day. All the ingredients are ripe and ready to go from garden to stockpot. You may need to wait until the day cools down a bit for optimum enjoyment, or crank up the air-conditioning in order to serve it. It will be worth it!

1	large poblano pepper, stemmed, halved, and seeded	
2	large jalapeños, stemmed, halved, and seeded	
6–8	tomatillos, husked and quartered	
3 tablespoons, divided	extra virgin olive oil	45 g
2 teaspoons, divided	kosher salt	12 g
1	large carrot, chopped	
2	ribs celery, chopped	
1	white onion, chopped	
1½ cups	summer ale	340 g
4 cups	reduced-sodium vegetable broth	907 g
1 (15.5-ounce) can	hominy, rinsed and drained	439 g
1 teaspoon	minced fresh mint leaves	0.5 g
1 teaspoon	minced fresh oregano leaves	0.5 g
1 teaspoon	freshly ground black pepper	3 g
1 teaspoon	garlic powder	2 g
½ teaspoon	ground cumin	2 g

GARNISHES

¼ head	green cabbage, thinly sliced	
1	large tomato, chopped	
1	large avocado, peeled, pitted, and chopped	
½	large red onion, chopped	
½ cup	chopped fresh cilantro leaves	8 g
½ cup	crumbled cotija (optional)	75 g
½ cup	thinly sliced red radishes	27 g
2	large jalapeños, chopped	
2	limes, quartered	
for serving	tortilla chips	

Preheat the oven to 425°F.

Place the poblano, jalapeño, and tomatillo pieces, cut side down, on a rimmed baking sheet. Drizzle them with 1 tablespoon (15 g) of the olive oil and season them with 1 teaspoon (6 g) of the salt. Roast the vegetables for 10 minutes. Flip them, then roast them for an additional 10 minutes.

RECIPE CONTINUES ☞

ROASTED TOMATILLO, MINT, AND SUMMER ALE POZOLE

While the vegetables roast, start the soup. Heat the remaining 2 tablespoons (30 g) of olive oil in a large Dutch oven or stockpot over medium-high heat. Add the carrot, celery, and onion and cook, stirring occasionally, until the vegetables brown and start to caramelize, about 15 minutes. Add the beer, scraping the bottom of the pot to deglaze it. Stir in the broth.

Transfer the peppers and tomatillos and any accumulated juices to a blender. Add 1 cup of the soup to the blender and blend on high until smooth. Return the purée to the pot. Stir in the hominy, mint, oregano, black pepper, garlic powder, cumin, and remaining 1 teaspoon (6 g) of salt. Reduce the heat to medium and simmer the pozole for 30 minutes.

Taste and adjust the seasoning as needed. Serve with bowls of garnishes alongside, allowing guests to top their pozole as they wish.

HEIRLOOM TOMATO TART
WITH SUMMER ALE WHIPPED MASCARPONE

SERVES 4

I grow tomatoes in my garden specifically for this recipe. The warm, flavorful, juicy tomato against the buttery backdrop of a flaky tart crust and the tang of mascarpone make for the perfect summer meal. From appetizer to entrée, it's just about the best dish you can serve during the summer months.

DOUGH

1½ cups	all-purpose flour	180 g
1 teaspoon	kosher salt	6 g
2 tablespoons	granulated sugar	26 g
1 stick	unsalted butter, softened	114 g
3 tablespoons	unsalted butter, chilled and cut into small cubes	42 g
¼ cup	summer ale	57 g

FILLING

6 ounces	mascarpone	170 g
2 tablespoons	summer ale	28 g

ASSEMBLY

for dusting	all-purpose flour	
1–2	heirloom tomatoes, cut into ¼-inch slices	454 g
1 teaspoon	chopped fresh thyme leaves	0.5 g
1 teaspoon	chopped fresh oregano leaves	0.5 g
2 tablespoons	extra virgin olive oil	30 g
pinch	kosher salt	

TO MAKE THE DOUGH: Combine the flour, salt, sugar, and softened butter in the bowl of a food processor and process until smooth. Add the cold butter and pulse until the mixture is just combined. You will still be able to see some larger pieces of butter, which will create flaky layers. Pulse in the beer until it is completely incorporated. The dough will be very soft.

Lay a long sheet of plastic wrap on a work surface. Turn out the dough onto the plastic wrap and form it into a disk about 6 inches in diameter. Wrap the disk tightly in the plastic and refrigerate until firm, about 3 hours or up to 3 days.

TO MAKE THE FILLING: Put the mascarpone in the bowl of a stand mixer fitted with the whisk attachment; whip on high for several minutes, then slowly add the beer, a splash at a time, until well combined.

TO ASSEMBLE: Preheat the oven to 425°F. Line a rimmed baking sheet with parchment paper.

Lightly flour a clean, dry work surface. Turn out the dough and roll it into a rustic circle, about ⅛ inch thick. Transfer the dough to the prepared baking sheet.

Cover the center of the dough with the mascarpone filling, leaving the outer 2 inches bare. Top with the tomato slices in concentric circles. Lift the bare edges of the dough up and over the top of the filling. Transfer the tart to the freezer and freeze for 15 minutes.

In a small bowl, stir together the thyme, oregano, and olive oil. Remove the tart from the freezer and brush it with some of the herb oil. Season with the salt. Bake the tart for 24 minutes or until golden brown.

Transfer the tart to a serving platter and drizzle it with the remaining herb oil. Serve.

GOCHUJANG AND ISA SHAKSHUKA

Shakshuka is a traditional Israeli dish that pulls double duty as breakfast offering and evening entrée. With its bold and satisfying flavors, it's the culinary peak of breakfast for dinner. The gorgeous tomato sauce and the beautiful eggs with the still-runny yolks make it perfect any time of day. Kale (or chard) is used in the bright, summery dish because although it peaks in the spring, it's still available through the summer in abundance.

2–3	large ripe tomatoes	
2 tablespoons	extra virgin olive oil	30 g
½ cup	diced yellow onion	75 g
1	red bell pepper, seeded and diced	
1 cup	thinly sliced kale or Swiss chard	75 g
1 cup, divided	ISA	227 g
2 tablespoons	gochujang (Korean chili paste)	32 g
1 teaspoon	kosher salt	6 g
½ teaspoon	freshly ground black pepper	1.5 g
½ teaspoon	chili powder	1.5 g
½ teaspoon	garlic powder	1.5 g
½ teaspoon	smoked paprika	1.5 g
¼ teaspoon	ground cumin	1.5 g
6	large eggs	
for garnish	crumbled feta and chopped fresh flat-leaf parsley leaves	
for serving	pita, flatbread, or naan	

Put the tomatoes in a large heatproof bowl. Add enough water to completely submerge the tomatoes. Transfer just the water to a pot and bring to a rapid boil over high heat. Pour the boiling water back over the tomatoes. Allow the tomatoes to sit for 2 minutes, then drain them.

Remove and discard the tomato skins, then quarter the tomatoes. Remove and discard the seeds. Add the tomato flesh to a pot and bring to a simmer over medium-high heat, stirring and mashing with a potato masher until the tomato mixture is well crushed and slightly thickened, about 10 minutes. This can be done several days in advance (or months ahead of time, if the crushed tomatoes are canned properly or frozen).

Heat the oil in a large cast iron skillet over medium-high heat. Add the onion, bell pepper, and kale and cook until the pepper and kale are softened and the onion starts to show some color, about 10 minutes.

Stir in ¾ cup (170 g) of the beer. Simmer the vegetables until the beer is almost gone and the pan starts to look dry, about 10 minutes. Stir in the tomatoes, gochujang, salt, black pepper, chili powder, garlic powder, paprika, cumin, and remaining ¼ cup (57 g) of beer. Simmer until the mixture is slightly thickened, about 8 minutes.

Make six wells in the sauce, evenly spaced out across the pan. Crack 1 egg into each well.

Reduce the heat to medium-low, cover the pan partially, and simmer the shakshuka for 15 to 20 minutes, until the egg whites have set but the yolks are still soft.

Remove the pan from the heat. Garnish with feta and parsley and serve with your choice of bread.

NOTE

For quicker cooking, put the pan in a 350°F oven for 8 to 10 minutes, until the egg whites are cooked.

WATERMELON AND FETA SALAD
WITH BEER-PICKLED ONIONS

SERVES 4

Ever since I first tried watermelon seasoned with salt, I've never eaten it another way. I serve big, juicy wedges alongside a small dish filled with Hawaiian black salt. For something a bit more complex, I make this recipe, where the saltiness comes from beautiful feta cheese. It's the perfect way to enjoy one of summer's most delightful fruits. Be sure to start pickling the onions at least a day before you plan to serve the salad.

3 cups	cubed watermelon	907 g
1 cup	crumbled feta	57 g
¼ cup	chopped fresh cilantro leaves	6 g
2 tablespoons	extra virgin olive oil	30 g
1 tablespoon	freshly squeezed lemon juice	14 g
1 teaspoon	sea salt	6 g
½ teaspoon	chili powder	1.5 g
	Beer-Pickled Onions (recipe follows)	

In a serving bowl, toss together the watermelon, feta, and cilantro.

In a small bowl, whisk together the olive oil, lemon juice, salt, and chili powder. Drizzle the dressing over the watermelon salad.

Top with pickled onions as desired. Serve immediately.

≫ BEER-PICKLED ONIONS ≪

1½ cups	kölsch	340 g
1 cup	apple cider vinegar	240 g
1 tablespoon	granulated sugar	13 g
2 tablespoons	kosher salt	36 g
1 tablespoon	freshly ground black pepper	8 g
1	medium red onion, thinly sliced	

In a small saucepan, combine the beer, vinegar, sugar, salt, and pepper. Bring to a simmer over medium-high heat, and stir just until the sugar and salt dissolve. Remove the brine from the heat.

Put the onion slices in an airtight container. Pour the brine over the onion. Allow the onion to sit at room temperature until cooled, about 20 minutes. Cover and refrigerate for at least 1 day and for up to 1 week.

WATERMELON AND CUCUMBER BEER SANGRIA

SERVES 4

I once nearly assaulted a waiter in Spain. Possibly an exaggeration, unless you ask the waiter. My sister and I had traveled through the Costa del Sol to a small and exceedingly charming Spanish beach town. We'd ordered a pitcher of sangria and a few tapas to share. When the sangria arrived 45 minutes before the food, the alcohol took hold in an assertive way. I tried to ask where my food was in my toddler-like Spanish, but something got lost in translation. Luckily, the food finally arrived, and my sister and I became much kinder, gentler souls, making amends with the waiter. All in all, I'm not sure there is any other drink that gets me as animated as a good sangria.

2 cups	**watermelon balls**	350 g
½	**medium watermelon, rind removed, cubed**	
1 cup	**peeled cucumber slices**	150 g
4	**large fresh mint leaves, cut into ribbons**	
¼ cup	**granulated sugar**	50 g
1	**large lime, juiced**	
½ cup	**triple sec**	135 g
3¼ cups	**gose**	750 g

Put the watermelon balls in a freezer-safe container and freeze.

Put the watermelon cubes in a blender and blend until smooth. Allow the watermelon purée to sit until settled, about 20 minutes, then strain through a fine-mesh sieve to remove and discard the pulp. Transfer the watermelon juice (about 3 cups) to a large serving pitcher. Add the cucumber slices, mint, sugar, lime juice, and triple sec and stir to combine. Cover and refrigerate for at least 24 hours and up to 3 days.

When ready to serve, stir the beer into the pitcher and add the frozen watermelon balls.

FALL

/ fôl /

VERB: to descend freely by the force of gravity

NOUN: the season of the year referred to as autumn

———————

The first fall I spent in the Pacific Northwest was a revelation. The collective sigh of relief when the heat of summer was over and the glory of the fall had finally arrived was palpable. During an afternoon run along a rain-soaked back road, the trees flaunting a fresh coat of brilliantly colored leaves in saturated red-gold hues, the crisp air stinging my lungs to life as the sunlight peppered the trail, I finally realized what all the fuss was about. The fall has a magic to it, an indescribable beauty that you feel rather than see. It's a change that happens quickly, a transition that's much more sudden and extreme than when the other seasons dawn. It's mild but powerful, welcoming and soothing. It's by far my favorite time of year, and not just because of the way the air smells in the bright early evenings.

It's a crossover season for both food and beer, a time when you can play with the best that fall has to offer and the best that summer is still giving up. It's a moment in the year when the crisp kölsch of summer is just as welcome as the comforting malt base of a fall brown ale. It's a moment in time when both soup and salad make perfect sense, and it can all still be enjoyed with a fruit pie. The sun is still around, but it's mellowed enough to allow you the freedom of a long walk through the woods in a woolen sweater and cozy scarf.

FALL PRODUCE

 denotes vegan recipe or easy vegan adaptations given

CABBAGE

Cabbage is versatile if you know how to work with it. You can ferment it (hello, gorgeous kimchi), make coleslaw (I've even pickled coleslaw), wrap stuff in it (cabbage rolls, yum), and use it to beef up your salads or spring rolls, and it's even an excellent garnish for pozole. When selecting cabbage, look for a head that's tightly packed (leaves tend to loosen as they age) with a stem that's firm and not limp. Refrigerate in your crisper drawer until ready to use. While I tend to lean toward the napa and savoy varieties, there are plenty of types to play with. Cannonball cabbage is great for coleslaw, bok choy is perfect for stir-fry, and red cabbage is ideal for pickling and adding to salads.

CARROTS

While most of us grew up eating orange Imperator carrots, there are dozens of varieties out there. Most are hard to come by at typical grocery stores, but they are worth seeking out just to marvel at the variations available. Atomic Reds and Cosmic Purples, for example, are positively beautiful! All are fairly interchangeable when it comes to cooking, but the array of colors gives your dishes an extra pop. Don't neglect the greens! While buying carrots with the tops still attached will likely be an indicator that they are freshly harvested, you want to remove them ASAP. The greens will suck moisture out of the root (the carrot) and leave it limp. But once the top has been removed, don't toss 'em, use 'em. They are excellent in chimichurri or pesto recipes, or just tossed into your homemade vegetable stock.

CAULIFLOWER

Out of nowhere, cauliflower has gone from a forgotten little vegetable to the produce cool kid (move over, kale!). It's no wonder, since it can do so much—soup, pizza crust, rice substitute! When choosing your bounty at the market, look for firm heads without brown spots. A good rule of thumb is allowing for eight ounces per person, but a little extra never hurt anyone. Want to rice it? I don't blame you. The easiest ways to turn a head of cauliflower into a rice substitute are to grate it with a box grater or to pulse the florets in a food processor a few times.

CORN

Corn is a crossover vegetable (or is it a grain? or a fruit?), coming into season in the late summer but crossing over to peak just as fall begins. It's delicious fresh, cooked, grilled, and even dried and popped. You can make flour out of it, and even cake. There really isn't anything this little beast can't do, besides stay in a classification category! Did you know that peeling back the cornhusk in the market is bad corn-buying etiquette? Sure, you want to peek inside to see if it's good, but in doing so you remove the protective barrier that helps the kernels stay fresh and full of juice! Instead of doing the peel-and-peek, look for teensy holes in the husk (especially near the top); they could be wormholes and should be avoided. Feel the ears for plump kernels without empty spots in the cob, and opt for a corn silk tassel that is brown and sticky (not black or dry).

BRUSSELS SPROUTS

I was at the market buying Brussels sprouts one day, and the lady in front of me visibly cringed. "Ugh, I hate those," she said. I responded to the bag of sprouts as if to apologize to them: "That's because your mom boiled them until they were gray and made you eat them." She stared at me as if I were a witch, divining memories from her past. It's a common problem these little sprouts have had to fight, and it's not their fault that so many people prepare them the wrong way. Cook them right and you'll convert entire generations into sprout lovers. Seek out sprouts that are tight without yellow or black spots, and avoid overly large ones, as they tend to be older and more bitter.

FIGS

Figs start to make an appearance in late summer, gracing us with their beautiful juicy presence in July. By the time fall rolls around, the trees are fat with their dark purple teardrop bodies. Once fall is in full swing, the figs have taken over. Use them while you can, because the season ends quickly, and then these beautiful little fruits vanish for the year. My favorite way to preserve them is to dry them. Just set your oven on the lowest setting possible (around 145°F), space the figs out on a rimmed baking sheet, and put them in the oven. Turn them every few hours until they are dry to the touch but still pliable. It can take anywhere from 8 to 24 hours, depending on the size of the figs and the humidity in your kitchen. Store in an airtight container in a cool, dark place for up to 6 months.

GINGER

This gnarled root pulls double duty by offering its sweet-hot flavors to both sweet and savory dishes. Young ginger root, also known as spring ginger, is rare but can be sourced at some well-stocked Asian markets. Its skin is so thin and delicate that it doesn't require peeling like the mature ginger used in this book's recipes—mature ginger's hide is tough and needs to go. Use the tip of a spoon to scrape it away without losing any of the lovely flesh. Need another use for ginger? Add it to equal parts sugar and water, boil for a minute, and allow to cool. Strained and stored to use in cocktails, ginger simple syrup is a win any time of year!

HOPS

Rarer than diamonds, hops are little flowers that are essential to beer making, imparting a beautifully bitter flavor to the brew. When hops come into season, the craft beer world goes into a frenzy. Brewers fly to the Yakima Valley, Germany, and a few other prime locations to select the perfect hops. In fall, we get just a few weeks (months, if we're lucky) when beer made with hops fresh off the bine (the term for a hop vine) becomes available to the market. Since fresh hops are so rare, I call for dried hops in these recipes. Hops are usually picked from the bine, immediately kiln dried, and either turned into pellets or stored as dried flowers. Dried hops are easy to source at any homebrew store or online. For these recipes, I've used two of my favorite varieties that are also widely available: Citra and Cascade. Citra hops have bright, citrus, and tropical fruit flavors. Cascade hops tend to be earthier, with notes of pine, flowers, and a bit of citrus.

MUSHROOMS

Mushrooms have always been a favorite of mine, replacing meat when I was a vegetarian, and versatile enough to throw into most dishes. They are, however, in season all year. One variety or another is popping out of the ground during any month for your continued enjoyment. Morels peak in the spring, while oysters and black trumpets peak in winter. But fall brings you chanterelles, creminis, porcinis, and shiitakes. Fall is the king of mushroom foraging and cooking, so fall is where we'll put them. Mushrooms are best stored in a paper bag so they can breathe a bit and avoid accumulating moisture. Avoid airtight containers or plastic bags that promote deterioration.

PUMPKIN

The first time I made pumpkin purée was eye-opening. Cut, scoop, roast, purée, drain, done. I had so much to work with, and it freezes well. When choosing a pumpkin for eating, stick to pie pumpkins and steer away from the ones your kids carve faces into. While all pumpkin varieties are edible, not all varieties are *intended* to be eaten. The carving varieties are bred for looks and sturdiness, not flavor. Look for small pie pumpkins for use in both savory and sweet dishes. For these recipes, I tested with sugar pie pumpkins. They weigh about three pounds each and are found in the produce section rather than in boxes outside the grocery store at Halloween.

FALL BEERS

When the weather shifts to a cooler spectrum, the beer warms up. The malt becomes more pronounced, the hop bitterness mellows, and spices start to make an appearance. Fall beer (with the exception of fresh hop beer) is a transition from the crisp, hoppy bite of summer ales into the deep, roasty, heavy beers of winter. It's a time when brewers get creative and the spectrum of flavors is in full tilt.

PUMPKIN BEER. It's impossible to have a conversation about fall beer and not address the big orange elephant in the fermentation room. The popularity of this style has ebbed and flowed through the years, but one thing is certain: it's here to stay. From IPAs to stouts, brewers have pumpkined up every style you can pour into a pint glass. Most often these are beers that have a strong malt base, are spiced with cloves, allspice, or cinnamon, and have a lower hop profile and a higher ABV.

FRESH HOP BEER. Ask a craft beer fan what their favorite fall style is, and more often than not, it's the fresh hop beer. Also known as "wet hop," this is a style that is rare and fleeting, with a very small window of time to brew and enjoy. Hops, small green flowers that resemble tiny, soft green pine cones, are grown on vines (known as bines) that have only one harvest a year, in late summer. Most often the hops are dried and turned into pellets (or dried and kept as dried hop flowers) for later use. Once a hop is picked, it has less than twenty-four hours to either be used or be dried before it starts to mold. The vast majority of hops are grown near the forty-ninth parallel, in both the United States and Europe. Those brewers within driving distance of hop farms are the lucky winners of the proximity game, giving them the ability to brew with hops right off the bine, known as "fresh hops."

A few weeks later, in early fall, these beers are ready to consume. The oils in the fresh hops, known as lupulin, give the beer a unique and very distinct flavor. The very short window to brew these beers make them the belles of the ball when it comes to seasonal beer.

 BROWN ALE. Brown ale is malty, but not as much as a stout or porter, and it has a nice level of carbonation, but not as much as most IPAs. With brown ales, you still get that malty warmth, but with a lighter flavor and notes of nuts, bread, and caramel. It's a nice middle ground and a good transition as we move into rich winter beers. Don't forsake brown ale as the weather turns colder, as it's a great beer for winter as well. The flavors and carbonation are just right to cut the richness of winter foods.

 OKTOBERFEST. Oktoberfest begins in Germany at the end of September, right as fall is beginning. Oktoberfest and "Oktoberfest-style" beers (known as märzen beers) are made specifically for the celebration. They're most often lagers, with a rich amber color, malty sweetness, and a lower hop profile. The term "Oktoberfest" is technically a registered trademark of breweries inside Munich city limits—those breweries are the only ones that can label their beer "Oktoberfest." Everyone else must say "Oktoberfest style."

 BELGIAN DUBBEL. Dubbels got their name from the Belgian monks who invented the style in the 1800s. The dark beer is made to be about double the strength of the everyday beer the monks were drinking, putting its ABV somewhere around 8 percent, a bit less than either a quad or a tripel. They're darker in color than the tripel, thanks to the use of caramelized sugar used in the brewing process. Expect notes of dark fruit, cloves, chocolate, nuts, and caramel—perfect flavors for fall beer. Dubbels make the quintessential Thanksgiving pairing beer, playing nice with everything from mashed potatoes and gravy to the mysterious green whipped cream "salad" your aunt insists on bringing.

BLACK BEAN AND FARRO
STUFFED CABBAGE ROLLS
WITH BROWN ALE AND TAMARIND SAUCE

SERVES 4

*I like to wrap things in other things. It's like you're serving up a secret, or a present, or a burrito.
And everyone likes a secret burrito present, am I right? The magic in these little cabbage rolls
is how delicious they are. Tamarind is the podlike offering of a tropical tree; its sweet-sour
warmth is perfect with both a stout and the flavors of cabbage, farro, and black beans.*

2½ cups	**water**	565 g
pinch	**kosher salt**	
⅓ cup	**pearled farro**	66 g
1	**large head savoy cabbage, leaves removed**	
1 (15-ounce) can	**black beans, rinsed and drained**	425 g
1	**large carrot, finely grated**	
1 teaspoon	**garlic powder**	3 g
½ teaspoon	**kosher salt**	3 g
2 cups	**reduced-sodium vegetable broth**	472 g
	Brown Ale and Tamarind Sauce (recipe follows)	

Bring the water to a boil over high heat. Season with salt. Stir in the farro and reduce the heat to medium-low. Cover and simmer for 30 minutes or until the farro is soft and chewy. Drain the farro, transfer it to a large bowl, and set it aside.

Bring a large pot of water to a boil over medium-high heat. Add the cabbage leaves, a few at a time, and cook just long enough to soften the leaves, about

2 minutes. Using tongs, transfer the softened leaves to paper towels to drain. Repeat this process until all the cabbage leaves have been softened and drained. Drain the pot and return it to the stove off the heat.

Add the black beans, carrot, garlic powder, and salt to the farro. Mash the mixture with a potato masher until the beans are mostly mashed and well combined with the farro.

Working with one cabbage leaf at a time, spoon about 3 tablespoons of the filling in a line down the center of the leaf. Fold the short sides in over the filling, then flap one of the long ends over the filling and roll tightly. Place the roll, seam side down, in the pot. Repeat until you've used all the filling. Pour the broth into the pot, cover, and bring to a boil over medium-high heat. Reduce the heat to medium and simmer for 10 minutes or until the cabbage is tender.

Transfer the cabbage rolls to a paper towel–lined plate to drain for a few minutes, then arrange them on a serving plate. Serve the cabbage rolls alongside the sauce for dipping.

RECIPE CONTINUES ☞

BLACK BEAN AND FARRO STUFFED CABBAGE ROLLS WITH BROWN ALE AND TAMARIND SAUCE

CONTINUED

⇒ BROWN ALE AND TAMARIND SAUCE ⇐

3 tablespoons	brown ale	42 g
2 tablespoons	reduced-sodium soy sauce	30 g
2 tablespoons	tamarind paste	32 g
2 tablespoons	creamy peanut butter	32 g
2 tablespoons, packed	golden brown sugar	28 g
1	clove garlic, grated	
1 teaspoon	red pepper flakes	3 g

In a small bowl, whisk together all the ingredients until smooth. Use right away or store in an airtight container in the refrigerator for 3 days.

ROASTED CABBAGE WEDGES
WITH FETA-MUSTARD BEER VINAIGRETTE

Who ever heard of roasting salad?! It's so strange and so unexpected, but it turns out it's delicious.
I intended it as a side dish, but once you dig in, you may be tempted to make it the main event.

CABBAGE

1	large head savoy cabbage	
2 tablespoons	extra virgin olive oil	30 g
½ teaspoon	kosher salt	3 g
½ teaspoon	freshly ground black pepper	2 g

VINAIGRETTE

¼ cup	Belgian dubbel	57 g
¼ cup	freshly squeezed lemon juice	56 g
¼ cup	extra virgin olive oil	60 g
2 teaspoons	mustard powder	3 g
1 teaspoon	kosher salt	6 g
⅓ cup	crumbled feta	57 g

TO MAKE THE CABBAGE: Preheat the oven to 425°F.

Halve the cabbage lengthwise. Then cut each half in half lengthwise, then in half lengthwise again. This will give you 8 equal wedges. Arrange the wedges, cut side down, on a rimmed baking sheet. Drizzle them with the olive oil and season with the salt and pepper.

Roast the cabbage in the bottom third of the oven for 15 minutes. Flip the wedges onto the other cut side and roast for an additional 15 minutes.

TO MAKE THE VINAIGRETTE: Whisk together the beer, lemon juice, olive oil, mustard powder, and salt. Stir in the crumbled feta.

Transfer the roasted cabbage wedges to a serving platter. Drizzle them with vinaigrette as desired. Serve.

ROASTED
CABBAGE
WEDGES

PAGE 141

HONEY AND ALE ROASTED CARROT TART
WITH CARROT GREEN PESTO

SERVES 6

Did you know that you can make pesto sauce with the greens from the tops of carrots? It's really too bad that they so often get cut off before they get to your local market, but a good carrot pesto will make you search for those Bugs Bunny–style carrots with the ridiculously long leaves. They're fun and functional.

6–8	rainbow carrots, with greens attached	
¼ cup	Oktoberfest beer	55 g
2 tablespoons	honey	42 g
6 tablespoons	extra virgin olive oil	90 g
½ teaspoon	kosher salt	3 g
for dusting	all-purpose flour	
1 (8-ounce) sheet	puff pastry, chilled but not frozen	
¼ cup	crumbled goat cheese	38 g
⅓ cup	fresh basil leaves (see Note)	6 g
1	large clove garlic, peeled and lightly smashed	
¼ cup	almonds	35 g
⅓ cup	shaved Parmigiano-Reggiano	30 g

Preheat the oven to 400°F. Set a wire rack in a rimmed baking sheet.

Cut the greens off the carrots, chop the greens, and reserve them for later. Quarter the carrots lengthwise and place them on the wire rack. In a small bowl, whisk together the beer, honey, 2 tablespoons (30 g) of the olive oil, and the salt until well combined. Brush the carrots with some of the honey mixture.

Transfer the wire rack and baking sheet to the oven. Roast the carrots for 15 minutes. Brush them again with the honey mixture, then roast for another 15 minutes or until tender. Remove the carrots from the oven, but keep it on.

Line another rimmed baking sheet with parchment paper, and lightly flour a clean, dry work surface. Using a rolling pin, roll out the puff pastry into a 12 × 10-inch rectangle. Transfer the pastry to the prepared baking sheet. Lightly score a 1-inch border around the pastry's edges. Scatter the crumbled goat cheese all over the middle of the pastry, up to the 1-inch border. Add the carrots in tight rows on top of the goat cheese. Bake for 15 to 18 minutes, until the puff pastry is golden brown.

In the bowl of a food processor, combine ½ cup (37 g) of the reserved chopped carrot greens (reserve the rest for another use), the basil, the garlic, the almonds, and the Parmigiano-Reggiano. Process the mixture until well combined. With the machine running, slowly add the remaining 4 tablespoons (60 g) of olive oil through the feed tube and blend to combine the pesto.

Drizzle the tart with pesto as desired (transfer the rest to an airtight container and store in the fridge for up to 1 week). Cut into squares and serve.

NOTE

Basil season ends in early fall. If you have a hard time sourcing basil, flat-leaf parsley is in season and makes an excellent stand-in.

BROWN SUGAR AND OKTOBERFEST GLAZED CARROTS

No offense to the orange guys, but rainbow carrots are just more fun. From white to purple, they can run around the color spectrum. It makes you wonder why you don't see more diversity in the produce aisle. Although, if all you can find are the traditional pumpkin-hued Imperator carrots, those will do just fine.

¼ cup	**Oktoberfest beer**	57 g
2 tablespoons	**apple cider vinegar**	30 g
¼ cup, packed	**golden brown sugar**	55 g
1 teaspoon	**kosher salt**	6 g
pinch	**cayenne pepper**	
6–8	**large rainbow carrots, quartered lengthwise (and halved crosswise if long)**	
1 teaspoon	**chopped fresh thyme leaves**	0.5 g

Combine the beer, vinegar, brown sugar, salt, and cayenne in a small saucepan and bring to a boil over high heat. Cook, stirring occasionally, until the mixture thickens, about 2 minutes.

Reduce the heat to medium. Stir in the carrots, making sure all the carrots are coated. Cover and simmer for about 5 minutes, until the carrots are softened.

Transfer the carrots to a serving plate. Drizzle them with any sauce left in the pan. Sprinkle them with the thyme and serve warm.

CURRIED CAULIFLOWER
AND BROWN ALE PANANG

SERVES 4

After a long day of travel, when I'm safely back home and my unpacked suitcase sits in my closet being ignored, I always want to order in Thai food. Panang is my favorite. I love it extra spicy with as many vegetables as the restaurant has. For this home-style version, feel free to add mushrooms, potatoes, or even butternut squash if the mood strikes.

2 cups	water	460 g
1 teaspoon, divided	kosher salt	6 g
1 cup	long-grain white rice	180 g
2 tablespoons	extra virgin olive oil	30 g
1	small head cauliflower, cut into florets	
2 (13.5-ounce) cans	full-fat coconut milk	772 g
1 cup	brown ale	227 g
⅓ cup	red curry paste	80 g
1 teaspoon	Sriracha	5 g
1 teaspoon	tamarind paste	5 g
1 teaspoon	freshly ground black pepper	5 g
1 teaspoon	chopped fresh sage leaves	0.5 g
½ teaspoon	chopped fresh thyme leaves	0.25 g
1	medium roasted red bell pepper (store-bought or homemade), chopped	

In a small saucepan, bring the water to a boil over high heat. Season the water with ½ teaspoon (3 g) of the salt, stir in the rice, cover, and reduce the heat to low. Cook for 20 minutes. Remove the pan from the heat, fluff the rice with a fork, and set it aside.

Heat the olive oil in a large pot over medium-high heat. Add the cauliflower and cook, stirring occasionally, for 3 to 4 minutes, until the florets start to brown slightly.

Stir in the coconut milk, beer, curry paste, Sriracha, tamarind, remaining ½ teaspoon (3 g) of salt, the black pepper, the sage, the thyme, and the roasted red pepper. Bring the mixture to a low simmer and cook, stirring occasionally, until the cauliflower has softened but is still slightly firm, about 10 minutes.

Serve the panang over the rice.

ROASTED CAULIFLOWER
WITH CREAMY BEER AND LEEK SAUCE

Roast up some cauliflower and you'll have no idea what the haters are talking about. The mild and slightly nutty flavor is perfect in so many dishes. Serve it with a creamy leek sauce, and dunk to your heart's content. Leeks bring a bright, sweet, pleasantly oniony flavor that balances beautifully with the cauliflower. While leeks peak in winter (check out the winter chapter for more leek celebration!), they begin their season in fall.

1	large head cauliflower, cut into florets	
2 tablespoons	extra virgin olive oil	30 g
1 teaspoon, divided	kosher salt	6 g
1 teaspoon, divided	freshly ground black pepper	4 g
1 tablespoon	unsalted butter	14 g
2	large leeks (see Note on page 202), white and light green parts only, chopped	
¼ cup	Belgian dubbel	57 g
¼ cup	half-and-half	60 g
¼ cup	reduced-sodium vegetable broth	60 g

Preheat the oven to 425°F.

Scatter the cauliflower florets on a rimmed baking sheet. Drizzle with the olive oil, ½ teaspoon of the salt, and ½ teaspoon of the pepper, tossing to coat. Roast until a fork easily pierces the cauliflower, about 35 minutes.

Melt the butter in a sauté pan over medium heat. Add the leeks and cook until tender, about 8 minutes. Stir in the beer, half-and-half, broth, remaining ½ teaspoon of salt, and remaining ½ teaspoon of pepper. Simmer until the sauce thickens, about 6 minutes.

Transfer to a blender, allow to cool slightly, and blend until smooth.

Transfer the cauliflower to a serving dish. Drizzle it with the sauce if desired or serve it on the side for dipping.

BLACK BEAN AND GRILLED CORN SALAD
WITH QUESO FRESCO AND FRESH HOP DRESSING

SERVES 4

When summer spills into fall and the weather is still warm enough, the last gasps of summer produce still linger in the market, but the early fall offerings, such as fresh hop beer and corn on the cob, have started to show their faces. This recipe is the perfect way to celebrate. The early fall is one of the best times of year for both weather and produce.

SALAD

2	ears yellow corn, husk and silk removed	
1	large red bell pepper	
2 tablespoons	extra virgin olive oil	30 g
1 teaspoon	kosher salt	6 g
1 teaspoon	freshly ground black pepper	4 g
1 (15-ounce) can	black beans, rinsed and drained	425 g
2 tablespoons	chopped fresh cilantro leaves	2 g
2 tablespoons	crumbled queso fresco	28 g

DRESSING

¾ cup	crumbled queso fresco	142 g
2 tablespoons	apple cider vinegar	30 g
3 tablespoons	fresh hop beer	43 g
¼ cup	chopped fresh cilantro leaves	4 g
1 teaspoon	honey	7 g
½ teaspoon	garlic powder	1.5 g
½ teaspoon	chili powder	1.5 g
½ teaspoon	kosher salt	3 g

TO MAKE THE SALAD: Prepare a charcoal grill for direct heat or heat a gas grill to medium-high.

Drizzle the ears of corn and the bell pepper with the olive oil and season with the salt and pepper. Place the corn and bell pepper on the cooking grate and grill until grill marks appear on all sides, about 3 minutes per side.

Cut the kernels off the cob. Chop the bell pepper into bite-size pieces; discard the stem, seeds, and ribs. In a large bowl, toss together the corn, bell pepper, beans, cilantro, and queso fresco.

TO MAKE THE DRESSING: In a blender, combine the queso fresco, vinegar, beer, cilantro, honey, garlic powder, chili powder, and salt. Blend on high until the dressing is creamy.

Add the dressing as desired to the salad, tossing to coat. Serve.

MEXICAN STREET CORN BEER CAKES
WITH CHIPOTLE CREMA

I used to live near Echo Park in Los Angeles. One of the best snacks you could grab yourself on a summer afternoon was elote, or Mexican street corn, from the vendor who circled the lake with his little cart. For just a few dollars you got an ear of grilled corn smeared with all the toppings. I defy anyone to try one of his treats and not want to go home and make every imaginable version it.

CAKES

2	ears yellow corn, husk and silk removed	
½ cup	cornmeal	60 g
¼ cup	all-purpose flour	30 g
½ teaspoon	smoked paprika	1.5 g
1	large egg, lightly beaten	
1 tablespoon	chopped green onion (light green and white parts only)	5 g
½ cup	cotija	70 g
1 tablespoon	chopped fresh cilantro leaves	1 g
¼ cup	fresh hop beer	57 g
½ teaspoon	kosher salt	3 g
½ teaspoon	freshly ground black pepper	2 g
1 tablespoon	extra virgin olive oil	15 g

SAUCE

2 cups	Mexican crema	460 g
2 tablespoons	chopped chipotle in adobo	34 g
½ teaspoon	kosher salt	3 g
½ teaspoon	garlic powder	1.5 g

TO MAKE THE CAKES: Cut the corn kernels off the cobs. You should get about 2 cups (250 g). Put them in a large bowl and add the cornmeal, all-purpose flour, smoked paprika, egg, green onion, cotija, cilantro, beer, salt, and pepper. Stir until combined.

With wet hands, measure about ¼ cup of the dough and form it into a 1-inch-thick patty. Place the patty on a plate or baking sheet. Repeat with the remaining dough.

Heat the oil in a skillet over medium-high heat. Cook the patties on each side until golden brown, about 3 minutes per side.

TO MAKE THE SAUCE: In a bowl, stir together the crema, chipotle, salt, and garlic powder.

Serve the corn cakes with the sauce on the side or drizzled on top.

MIRIN AND ALE CARAMELIZED BRUSSELS SPROUTS
WITH GOAT CHEESE AND POMEGRANATE

SERVES 4

I have a hard time imagining Brussels sprout dishes that don't include both goat cheese and pomegranates—the flavors just go so well together. This particular example is one of my favorites and could easily be my go-to side dish for almost all cool-weather occasions.

2 tablespoons	**extra virgin olive oil**	30 g
6 cups	**halved Brussels sprouts**	454 g
¼ cup	**mirin**	70 g
¼ cup	**fresh hop beer**	57 g
½ teaspoon	**red pepper flakes**	0.5 g
½ teaspoon	**kosher or sea salt**	3 g
¼ cup	**crumbled goat cheese**	38 g
¼ cup	**pomegranate seeds (see Note)**	60 g

Heat the olive oil in a large skillet over high heat. Add the Brussels sprouts, cut side down, and cook until the they start to brown, about 6 minutes.

Add the mirin, beer, and red pepper flakes. Cook, stirring occasionally, until the pan is almost dry, about 4 minutes.

Transfer the Brussels sprouts to a serving dish. Season with the salt. Sprinkle the sprouts with the goat cheese and pomegranate seeds. Serve immediately.

NOTE

If seeding a pomegranate seems intimidating, you're not alone. In fact, most grocery stores sell little packages of just the seeds for anyone not willing to tackle the entire beast. To remove the seeds from a whole fruit, score a line around the center (just to cut the skin but not the inner seeds). Pull the halves apart. Over a small bowl, push to invert the halves, popping the seeds out. Fill the bowl with water to separate the papery membranes from the seeds.

MIRIN AND ALE
CARAMELIZED
BRUSSELS SPROUTS

PAGE 155

BRUSSELS
SPROUT LEAF
PIZZA

——

PAGE 158

BRUSSELS SPROUT LEAF PIZZA
WITH BEER-CARAMELIZED ONION

SERVES 4

Brussels sprouts give this pizza a distinctively fall flavor. Add the sweetness of the caramelized onions and the creaminess of the ricotta cheese and you might not make another type of pizza for the rest of the season. If you want to cut down on prep time the day of, make the onions several days in advance and store them in an airtight container in the fridge.

DOUGH

2½ cups	bread flour	318 g
1 (2¼-teaspoon) packet	fast-rising instant yeast	
1 teaspoon	granulated sugar	5 g
½ teaspoon	garlic powder	1.5 g
¾ cup	Oktoberfest beer	170 g
½ teaspoon	kosher salt	3 g
¼ cup	extra virgin olive oil	60 g

ONION

2 tablespoons	unsalted butter	28 g
1	medium sweet white onion, thinly sliced	
1 tablespoon, packed	golden brown sugar	14 g
1 teaspoon	kosher salt	6 g
1 cup	Oktoberfest beer	227 g

ASSEMBLY

8	large Brussels sprouts	
2 tablespoons	extra virgin olive oil	30 g
for dusting	semolina flour or cornmeal	
¼ cup	marinara or red pizza sauce	56 g
¼ cup	ricotta	60 g
4 ounces	fresh mozzarella, sliced	113 g

TO MAKE THE DOUGH: In the bowl of a stand mixer fitted with the dough hook attachment, mix the flour, yeast, sugar, and garlic powder on medium speed until combined.

Put the beer in a microwave-safe bowl. Microwave on high for 20 seconds. Test the beer's temperature with an instant-read thermometer and repeat this process until it registers between 120°F and 125°F or reaches the temperature specified on the package of yeast.

Add the beer to the flour mixture and mix on medium speed until most of the flour has been moistened. With the mixer running, slowly add the salt and oil. Increase the speed to high and beat the dough until it is smooth and elastic, about 8 minutes.

Lightly grease a large bowl. Transfer the dough to the bowl and cover it tightly with plastic wrap. Allow the dough to sit in a warm place until it has doubled in size, 45 to 60 minutes.

TO MAKE THE ONION: In a saucepan, melt the butter over medium heat, then stir in the onion, brown sugar, and salt. Cook, stirring occasionally, until the onion starts to soften, about 15 minutes. Add the beer and simmer, stirring occasionally, until the beer is mostly gone. This will take at least 45 minutes, but it could take up to 2 hours. Watch the heat carefully, adjusting from medium to low if necessary to prevent the onion from burning. Set the caramelized onion aside.

TO ASSEMBLE: Place a pizza stone in the oven and preheat the oven to 475°F.

Remove the stems from the sprouts and discard. Remove the leaves, reserving the centers for another use. Put the leaves in a bowl and add 1 tablespoon (14 g) of the olive oil, tossing to coat the leaves.

Dust a pizza peel and a clean, dry work surface with semolina flour or cornmeal. Turn out the dough onto the work surface and roll it into a 10-inch circle. Transfer it to the prepared pizza peel. Top the dough with the marinara, then add the caramelized onion in an even layer.

Add the ricotta in small dollops all over the pizza. Add the mozzarella in a single layer. Add the Brussels sprout leaves in a single layer. Brush the exposed crust with the remaining 1 tablespoon (14 g) of olive oil.

Carefully transfer the pizza to the pizza stone in the oven. Bake until golden brown, about 12 minutes. Remove the pizza from the oven, slice, and serve.

NOTE

If you have an interest in homemade pizza endeavors, invest in a pizza stone and pizza peel. The heat from a preheated pizza stone is the best way to cook a crust, and it's nearly impossible to transfer the dough to the heated stone without a peel. If you don't have a baking stone, simply assemble the pizza on a baking sheet (rectangular pizza tastes just as good!) and put it in the oven. Your crust won't be as "restaurant quality," but the flavors will still be there.

COCONUT-FIG FRENCH TOAST CASSEROLE

SERVES 6

Here's how we can eat bread pudding for breakfast. We all know it's really dessert, but we're serving it with syrup and coffee, so it must be breakfast! We collectively nod along as we eat our dessert first, but sometimes that's exactly what you need to do. The candy-like sweetness of the figs adds a surprisingly beautiful, new flavor and texture to an old classic, making you wonder why figs aren't a staple in all your dessert-for-breakfast endeavors.

1 (1-pound)	challah loaf, cut into cubes	
20	black Mission figs, cut into quarters	
1 cup	whole milk	240 g
¾ cup	Belgian dubbel	170 g
1 (13.5-ounce) can	full fat coconut milk, shaken	
1 cup, packed	golden brown sugar	200 g
6	large eggs	
1 teaspoon	pure vanilla extract	5 g
1 teaspoon	kosher salt	6 g
¼ cup	dried coconut flakes	20 g
for serving	whipped cream or pure maple syrup	

Preheat the oven to 325°F. Lightly grease a 9 × 13-inch baking dish.

Arrange the bread cubes in an even layer in the prepared baking dish. Scatter the fig quarters evenly over the bread.

In a mixing bowl, whisk together the milk, beer, coconut milk, brown sugar, eggs, vanilla, and salt. Pour the mixture over the bread and figs, pressing down on the bread to make sure it is all submerged. Sprinkle the coconut flakes evenly over the casserole.

Cover the baking dish with aluminum foil and allow to sit at room temperature for 20 minutes to allow the bread to absorb the egg mixture (alternatively, you can refrigerate the casserole overnight before baking).

Bake for 35 minutes, then remove the foil and bake for an additional 20 to 25 minutes, until the center has puffed and the top has lightly browned.

Allow to cool slightly, then slice and serve with whipped cream or maple syrup.

BROWN ALE BAKLAVA
WITH BAKED BRIE AND FIGS

For something that sounds so fancy, this is an extraordinarily easy dish to make. The figs and the nut mixture can be made in advance (transfer them to airtight containers; store the figs in the fridge and the nuts at room temperature). In addition to the traditional butter used to brush onto phyllo when making baklava, we add a bit of beer. The beer bakes off, leaving a crispier phyllo crust than any baklava you've had before.

6	medium black Mission figs, quartered (see Note)	
¼ cup	walnut halves	30 g
¼ cup	shelled pistachios	33 g
2 tablespoons	golden brown sugar	25 g
1 teaspoon	ground cinnamon	2 g
2 tablespoons	unsalted butter, melted	28 g
4 tablespoons, divided	brown ale	57 g
¼ cup	honey, warmed	84 g
5 sheets	frozen phyllo dough, thawed overnight in refrigerator	
1 (8-ounce) wheel	brie	227 g
for serving	crackers or toasted bread	

Preheat the oven to 425°F. Line a rimmed baking sheet with parchment paper.

Arrange the quartered figs in a single layer on the prepared baking sheet. Roast for 20 to 30 minutes, until the figs have darkened and shriveled. (Water content in figs varies wildly, so keep an eye on them to make sure they don't burn). Reduce the oven temperature to 375°F.

Combine the walnuts, pistachios, brown sugar, and cinnamon in the bowl of a food processor and process until the nuts resemble crumbs.

In a small bowl, stir together the melted butter and 2 tablespoons (28.5 g) of the beer. In another small bowl, stir together the honey and the remaining 2 tablespoons (28.5 g) of beer.

Line the baking sheet with fresh parchment paper. Place one sheet of phyllo dough on it and brush it with the butter mixture. Add a second layer on top and brush it with the butter mixture. Repeat with the remaining three phyllo sheets and butter mixture.

Place the brie wheel in the center of the phyllo sheets. Scatter the nut mixture over the top, then add the figs. Drizzle 2 tablespoons of the honey mixture over the figs.

Gently gather the edges of the phyllo up and over the brie to form a tight package. Brush the top with another 2 tablespoons of the honey mixture.

Bake for 25 minutes or until the phyllo is a dark golden brown. Transfer to a serving platter and drizzle with the remaining 2 tablespoons of honey mixture. Use a sharp cheese knife to cut into the round, and serve with crackers.

NOTE
Roasted fresh figs add a beautiful char and caramelized sweetness to this dish, but if you can find only dried (or want to use figs you've dehydrated yourself—see page 134), this recipe will work just as well. Simply skip the roasting step and start making the nut mixture.

BROWN SUGAR AND BROWN ALE GINGER BARS

Think of these bars as the fall-flavored version of a blondie—like gingerbread but softer, with a delicious chewiness. The beerified icing just puts them over the top. We use two types of ginger here: fresh ginger for the bright, sweet heat that we love so much, and a touch of ground ginger for the warmer flavors that can come only when the root has been ground and dried.

BARS

4 tablespoons	unsalted butter, softened	56 g
1 teaspoon	grated fresh ginger	1 g
1	large egg	
3 tablespoons	unsulfured molasses (not blackstrap; see Note)	63 g
½ cup, packed	golden brown sugar	110 g
⅓ cup	granulated sugar	66 g
1 teaspoon	pure vanilla extract	5 g
1½ cups	all-purpose flour	180 g
1 teaspoon	baking powder	4 g
1 teaspoon	kosher salt	6 g
½ teaspoon	ground ginger	1 g
½ teaspoon	ground cinnamon	1 g
¼ teaspoon	ground nutmeg	0.5 g
¼ cup	brown ale	57 g

ICING

2 cups	powdered sugar	270 g
¼ cup	brown ale	57 g

TO MAKE THE BARS: Preheat the oven to 350°F. Grease an 8 × 8-inch baking dish.

In the bowl of a stand mixer fitted with the paddle attachment, beat the butter and grated ginger on medium speed until well combined. Add the egg and beat until well combined. Add the molasses, brown and granulated sugars, and vanilla and beat on high speed until the batter is light and fluffy, about 5 minutes.

Turn off the mixer. Add the flour, baking powder, salt, ground ginger, cinnamon, and nutmeg. Using a wooden spoon, mix until just combined. Pour in the beer and mix until just combined.

Transfer the batter to the prepared baking dish and smooth the top. Bake for 25 to 30 minutes, until the top of the bars springs back when lightly touched. Set aside to cool to room temperature.

TO MAKE THE ICING: In a medium bowl, stir together the sugar and beer. Top the bars with the icing, cut into squares, and serve.

NOTE

Blackstrap molasses is what happens when you boil cane juice three times, removing nearly all the sugar until you have a black, bitter sludge. Dark, light, and unsulfured molasses are all fairly interchangeable and pleasantly sweet. Make sure never to use blackstrap in a recipe unless it's specifically called for.

GINGER BEER SCONES

When I say "ginger beer," I don't mean ginger beer. *I mean ginger and beer in the same delightful breakfast treat. The ginger is subtle but noticeable, and the scones are perfect with a little orange marmalade and a beer for an afternoon treat.*

DOUGH

3¼ cups + more for dusting	all-purpose flour	390+ g
¾ cup	granulated sugar	150 g
1 teaspoon	baking soda	6 g
½ teaspoon	baking powder	2 g
½ teaspoon	kosher salt	3 g
1 tablespoon	grated lemon zest	6 g
2 teaspoons	grated fresh ginger	10 g
½ cup	buttermilk	120 g
¼ cup	Oktoberfest beer	57 g
1 stick	unsalted butter, melted	114 g

TOPPING

1 tablespoon	Oktoberfest beer	14 g
1 tablespoon	granulated sugar	13 g
¼ teaspoon	kosher salt	1.5 g

TO MAKE THE DOUGH: Preheat the oven to 400°F. Line a rimmed baking sheet with parchment paper.

In a mixing bowl, stir together the flour, sugar, baking soda, baking powder, salt, lemon zest, and ginger. Add the buttermilk, beer, and melted butter. Using a fork, stir until the dough is just combined.

Flour a clean, dry work surface. Turn out the dough. Divide it into 2 equal pieces. Form each piece into a 1-inch-thick disk. Cut each disk into 6 equal wedges. Transfer the wedges to the prepared baking sheet.

TO TOP: Brush the top of each scone with the beer. Sprinkle with the sugar and salt.

Bake until the scones are lightly golden brown, about 18 minutes. Serve warm.

CITRA HOP AND BASIL PESTO

It's official: I've made pesto with everything. It began as it usually does, with pine nuts and basil, but then I started to branch out to parsley, cilantro, and pecans. Then it was pecorino and mimolette—I was unstoppable! I finally landed on hops, with their delightful bitterness and bold flavors, and my journey was complete. I'd pestoed everything, and it was worth it.

2	cloves garlic, peeled	
¾ cup	pecans	102 g
1½ cups, packed	fresh basil leaves (see Note)	24 g
2 tablespoons	dried Citra hop flowers (see Note)	22 g
¾ cup	grated Parmigiano-Reggiano	57 g
1 cup	extra virgin olive oil	240 g
to taste	kosher salt and freshly ground black pepper	

To blanch the garlic and mellow the flavor, bring a small saucepan of water to a boil over high heat. Drop the garlic cloves into the boiling water and boil for 1 minute. Remove the garlic cloves with a slotted spoon and immediately plunge them into a bowl filled with ice and water.

Lightly smash the garlic cloves and transfer them to the bowl of a food processor. Add the pecans, basil, hops, and Parmigiano-Reggiano and process until well combined. With the machine running, slowly add the oil through the feed tube until well combined. Season with salt and pepper to taste. Use right away or store in an airtight container in the refrigerator for up to 1 week.

NOTES

Basil season ends in early fall. If you have a hard time sourcing basil, flat-leaf parsley is in season and makes an excellent stand-in.

Dried hops can be purchased at any homebrew supply store or online. Look for whole dried flowers rather than pellets. If you are lucky enough to get your hands on fresh hops, allow them to air-dry for several days before using.

HOPSTA
(CASCADE HOP LINGUINE)

I made hopsta—what I call hop pasta—for the first time in a friend's kitchen, which was specially designed for her homemade pasta endeavors. The gorgeous herbal aroma of the hops turned the entire house into a dry-hopped oasis. We'd invited several people over for dinner before we'd even tasted the goods. Turns out, we'd overestimated the amount of hops needed, and the pasta was more of an edible IPA. Sure, you can add more than the tablespoon of hops called for here, but that's only if you really like highly bitter dinners. You can also try serving this with Citra Hop and Basil Pesto (page 168).

4	large eggs	
1 tablespoon	dried Cascade hop flowers (see Note on page 168)	11 g
4¼ cups	00 pasta flour	510 g
½ teaspoon + more to taste	kosher salt	3+ g
4 tablespoons	butter, melted	57 g
for serving	shaved Parmigiano-Reggiano	

Combine the eggs and hops in a blender or the bowl of a food processor. Blend until well combined. Transfer the egg mixture to the bowl of a stand mixer fitted with the paddle attachment. Add the flour and salt and mix on medium speed until well combined and the dough comes together, about 6 minutes.

Turn out the dough onto a clean, dry work surface. Knead it until it's smooth and elastic. Cover the dough with a clean kitchen towel and allow it to rest for 20 minutes.

Cut the dough into 4 equal sections. Form each piece of the dough into a long, ¼-inch-thick oval. Pass one piece of the dough through a pasta roller adjusted to its widest setting. Decrease the width of the pasta roller one notch and pass the dough through it again. Decrease the width of the pasta roller again and pass the pasta through it. Continue this process until the pasta is passed through at its second-thinnest setting. Repeat this process with the remaining three sections of dough.

To create noodles, pass the rolled pieces of dough, one at a time, through a linguine cutter. Transfer the linguine to a pasta drying rack or lay them flat on a baking sheet. Allow the linguine to dry for 15 minutes.

Bring a large pot of salted water to a boil over high heat. Add the linguine and cook until it's al dente, about 5 minutes. Drain the cooked linguine. Toss with the butter and Parmigiano-Reggiano and season with salt. Serve.

HONEY, BELGIAN DUBBEL, AND WILD MUSHROOM BANH MI

SERVES 4

Banh mi should be a command. But, in that case, it would be "banh me!" because once you've had a really great banh mi sandwich, you'll be tempted to yell orders at people until you get another one in your grubby little paws. A beautiful hybrid of French and Vietnamese cuisine, this soft baguette filled with fresh vegetables and a spicy sauce will quickly become a favorite.

1 pound	wild mushrooms, such as oyster, chanterelle, shiitake, and cremini, sliced	457 g
1½ cups	Belgian dubbel	340 g
¼ cup	reduced-sodium soy sauce	60 g
2 tablespoons	honey or agave	42 g
2 teaspoons	garlic powder	6 g
1 teaspoon	kosher salt	6 g
½ cup	sour cream, mayonnaise, or vegan mayonnaise	120 g
1 tablespoon	Sriracha	15 g
4	hoagie rolls	
1	medium English cucumber, thinly sliced	
2	large carrots, cut into matchsticks	
1	large jalapeño, thinly sliced	
½ cup, packed	chopped fresh cilantro leaves	8 g

Put the mushrooms in a large zip-top bag or shallow bowl. In a small bowl, stir together the beer, soy sauce, honey, garlic powder, and salt. Pour the mixture over the mushrooms, then seal the bag or cover the bowl. Set the mushrooms aside to marinate at room temperature for 1 hour or in the refrigerator for up to 24 hours.

Preheat the oven to 425°F. Line a rimmed baking sheet with aluminum foil.

Remove the mushrooms from the marinade and discard the marinade. Transfer the mushrooms to the prepared baking sheet. Bake for 10 minutes, stir the mushrooms, then bake for 10 more minutes. Continue to bake, turning every 10 minutes, until the mushrooms are dry and most of the liquid has evaporated, about 20 more minutes. Remove the mushrooms from the oven and preheat the broiler.

In a small bowl, stir together the sour cream and Sriracha. Set it aside.

Split the hoagie rolls. Place the rolls, cut side up, on another baking sheet. Broil until lightly toasted, about 2 minutes. Spread the Sriracha cream on the insides of the rolls. Add the mushrooms. Top with the cucumber, carrots, jalapeño, and cilantro. Serve immediately.

GRILLED BROWN ALE MARINATED MUSHROOM TACOS
WITH CORN SALSA

I debated when to offer mushroom recipes in this book since one variety or another comes into season nearly the entire year. In the end, they just feel like fall. They work well grilled and also pair perfectly with corn, cementing my idea that they should be eaten in autumn.

1	ear corn, husk and silk removed (see Note)	
1 tablespoon	extra virgin olive oil	15 g
1½ teaspoons, divided	kosher salt	8 g
1 teaspoon	freshly ground black pepper	
3	large portobello mushrooms, stemmed and cut into ½-inch slices	
1 cup	brown ale	227 g
3 tablespoons	balsamic vinegar	45 g
1 teaspoon	onion powder	3 g
1 teaspoon	garlic powder	3 g
¼ cup	chopped fresh cilantro leaves	6 g
¼ cup	chopped shallot	8 g
1 tablespoon	freshly squeezed lemon juice	6 g
¼ teaspoon	hot pepper sauce	1 g
¼ cup	Mexican crema	60 g
1 tablespoon	chopped chipotle in adobo	22 g
12	corn tortillas	

Prepare a charcoal grill for direct heat or heat a gas grill to medium-high.

Drizzle the corn with the olive oil and season with 1 teaspoon (6 g) of the salt and the pepper. Place the corn on the cooking grate and grill until grill marks appear on all sides, about 3 minutes per side, then set it aside to cool to room temperature.

Add the mushrooms to the grill and grill until both sides have grill marks and the mushrooms have softened and warmed through, about 3 minutes per side. Transfer the mushrooms to a large zip-top bag or shallow bowl.

In a small bowl, stir together the beer, vinegar, onion powder, garlic powder, and ¼ teaspoon (1 g) of salt. Pour the mixture over the mushrooms, then seal the bag or cover the bowl. Set the mushrooms aside to marinate at room temperature for 1 hour or in the refrigerator for up to 24 hours.

Cut the kernels off the cob and put them in a small bowl. Add the cilantro, shallot, remaining ¼ teaspoon (1 g) of salt, the lemon juice, and the hot pepper sauce and stir to combine. In a separate bowl, stir together the crema and chipotle in adobo.

Remove the mushrooms from the marinade and discard the marinade. Load each tortilla with some of the mushrooms. Top with the corn salsa and adobo crema. Serve.

NOTE
If you have a hard time finding fresh corn, use ¾ cup frozen corn, thawed and drained.

PUMPKIN LASAGNA

I hate to break it to you: there are people in this world who hate pumpkin things. I know, I know, it's upsetting. But I have a theory. I believe that most of these people don't actually hate pumpkin, per se, just sweet pumpkin things. They may have never tried a great savory pumpkin dish. I offer this pumpkin lasagna to solve the issue, so we can all live in squash-filled harmony.

1 pound	lasagna noodles	454 g
2 tablespoons + more for tossing	extra virgin olive oil	30+ g
1	large shallot, finely chopped (about ⅓ cup)	
5 cups	stemmed and chopped red chard	180 g
1	clove garlic, grated	
2 teaspoons, divided	kosher salt	12 g
2 teaspoons, divided	freshly ground black pepper	10 g
3 (15-ounce) cans	pumpkin purée	670 g
½ cup, divided	pumpkin ale	113 g
¼ cup	heavy cream	60 g
¼ teaspoon	freshly grated nutmeg	0.5 g
¼ teaspoon	cayenne pepper	0.5 g
¼ teaspoon	ground cumin	0.5 g
¼ teaspoon	ground cinnamon	0.5 g
2 (16-ounce) containers	ricotta	907 g
2	large eggs, lightly beaten	
3 cups, divided	freshly grated Parmigiano-Reggiano	227 g
8 ounces	fresh mozzarella, sliced	227 g

Preheat the oven to 400°F. Grease a 9 × 13-inch baking dish.

Bring a large pot of salted water to a boil over high heat. Add the lasagna noodles and boil until just before al dente, about 6 minutes. Drain the noodles and toss them with a bit of olive oil to prevent sticking.

In a large skillet, heat the olive oil over medium-high heat. Add the shallot and cook, stirring occasionally, until softened, about 5 minutes. Add the chard and cook until it starts to soften and wilt, about 3 minutes. Add the garlic, 1 teaspoon (6 g) of the salt, and 1 teaspoon (5 g) of the black pepper and cook until no moisture remains and the chard starts to get slightly crispy, about 8 minutes.

In a large bowl stir together the pumpkin purée, ¼ cup (56.5 g) of the beer, ½ teaspoon (3 g) of the salt, and ½ teaspoon (2.5 g) of the black pepper. Add the heavy cream, nutmeg, cayenne, cumin, and cinnamon and stir until well combined.

In another bowl, stir together the ricotta, eggs, remaining ½ teaspoon (3 g) of salt, remaining ½ teaspoon (2.5 g) of black pepper, remaining ¼ cup (56.5 g) of beer, and 2 cups (151 g) of the Parmigiano-Reggiano.

Spread a thin layer of the pumpkin mixture in the prepared baking dish. Then add a layer of cooked noodles, overlapping them slightly. Add a layer of the ricotta mixture, then a sprinkle of the chard. Repeat the process until all the ingredients are used, making sure to end with a layer of noodles on top.

Sprinkle the top of the lasagna with the remaining 1 cup (76 g) of Parmigiano-Reggiano. Add the mozzarella slices in a single layer.

Cover the dish with aluminum foil and bake the lasagna for 30 minutes. Remove the foil and cook for an additional 10 minutes or until the center is warmed through and the cheese has browned on top.

ROASTED PUMPKIN GALETTE
WITH MÄRZEN-CARAMELIZED ONION,
BRUSSELS SPROUTS, AND POMEGRANATE

SERVES 4

Notice a theme here? I offer you another savory pumpkin dish in my mission to provide all the pumpkin lovers with delightful entrées to combat the pumpkin haters of the world. That, and I think we really do have enough traditional pumpkin pie recipes to go around. However, we can never have enough recipes that allow you to eat dinner and pie crust at the same time. The onions can be made several days in advance. Store them in an airtight container in the fridge until ready to use.

ONION

2 tablespoons	**unsalted butter**	28 g
1	**medium sweet white onion, sliced**	
1 tablespoon, packed	**golden brown sugar**	14 g
1 teaspoon	**kosher salt**	6 g
1 cup	**märzen**	227 g

DOUGH

1½ cups	**all-purpose flour**	180 g
1 teaspoon	**kosher salt**	6 g
2 tablespoons	**granulated sugar**	26 g
6 tablespoons	**unsalted butter, softened**	84 g
3 tablespoons	**unsalted butter, chilled and cut into small cubes**	42 g
¼ cup	**Belgian dubbel**	57 g

FILLING

1	**medium pie pumpkin**	
¼ cup	**märzen**	57 g
¼ teaspoon	**chopped fresh rosemary leaves**	0.5 g
¼ teaspoon	**chopped fresh thyme leaves**	0.5 g
½ teaspoon	**kosher salt**	3 g
½ teaspoon	**garlic powder**	1.5 g

ASSEMBLY

5	**large Brussels sprouts**	
2 tablespoons, divided	**extra virgin olive oil**	30 g
for dusting	**all-purpose flour**	
2 tablespoons	**pomegranate seeds (see Note on page 155)**	30 g
¼ cup	**crumbled goat cheese**	38 g

TO MAKE THE ONION: Melt the butter in a sauté pan over medium heat. Add the onion and cook, stirring occasionally, until it softens, about 5 minutes. Make sure the butter is not too hot or the onion will burn before it caramelizes. If the onion starts to darken too fast, or the butter is smoking, reduce the heat. Stir in the brown sugar, salt, and beer. Reduce the heat to medium-low and cook, stirring occasionally, until the onion is dark brown and the beer is mostly gone, 45 minutes to 1 hour. Remove the pan from the heat and set aside.

TO MAKE THE DOUGH: Combine the flour, salt, sugar, and softened butter in the bowl of a food processor. Process until the mixture is smooth. Add the cold butter and pulse until the mixture is just combined. You will still be able to see some larger pieces of butter, which will create flaky layers. Pulse

RECIPE CONTINUES ☞

in the beer until it is completely incorporated. The dough will be very soft.

Lay a long sheet of plastic wrap on a work surface. Turn out the dough onto the plastic wrap and form it into a disk about 6 inches in diameter. Wrap the disk tightly in the plastic and refrigerate until firm, about 3 hours and up to 3 days.

TO MAKE THE FILLING: Preheat the oven to 375°F. Line a rimmed baking sheet with aluminum foil.

Remove the stem of the pumpkin by running a butter knife around its edges and then prying it out.

Halve the pumpkin lengthwise, through the hole left by the stem. Scoop out the seeds. Discard them or save them for a future use.

Place the pumpkin halves, cut side down, on the prepared baking sheet. Cover tightly with aluminum foil. Roast for 1 to 1½ hours, until a fork can easily pierce the pumpkin's skin.

Remove the pan from the oven and set aside until the pumpkin is cool enough to handle. Scoop the flesh from both halves and put it in the bowl of a food processor. Process the pumpkin for a few minutes, until it's smooth. Transfer the pumpkin purée to a fine-mesh strainer and allow it to drain for 10 minutes to remove excess moisture.

Measure out 2 cups (244 g) of the pumpkin purée and put it in a bowl. (Reserve the rest for another use—pumpkin purée freezes well! Put it in a zip-top plastic bag and freeze for up to 1 month.) Add the beer, rosemary, thyme, salt, and garlic powder and stir to combine. Set it aside.

TO ASSEMBLE: Remove the stems from the sprouts and discard. Remove the leaves, reserving the centers for another use. Transfer the leaves to a bowl. Add 1 tablespoon (15 g) of the olive oil, tossing to coat the leaves.

Line a rimmed baking sheet with parchment paper. Flour a clean, dry work surface. Turn out the dough and roll it into a large circle about ¼ inch thick. Transfer the dough to the prepared baking sheet.

Spread the pumpkin filling in the center of the dough, leaving the outer 2 inches bare. Add the caramelized onion on top of the pumpkin in an even layer and top with the Brussels sprout leaves. Fold the crust borders over the filling to form a rustic circle. Brush the exposed crust with the remaining 1 tablespoon (15 g) of oil.

Bake in the lower third of the oven for 18 to 22 minutes, until the crust has turned golden brown. If the sprout leaves start to brown too quickly, cover the galette with foil.

Remove the galette from the oven. Top it with the pomegranate seeds and goat cheese. Slice and serve immediately.

WINTER

/ win(t)ər /

VERB: to endure a period of inactivity

NOUN: the coldest season of the year

Winter brings a wide spectrum of experience, from the highs of the holiday season, the New Year's celebrations, and ski vacations, to the lows of dark, short days and a long, cold January. The highs seem to balance out the lows in a way that makes it one of the most enjoyable seasons of the year. The cold days are the groundwork for the beauty of fresh snowfall. Short days just leave more time for evening cocktails by the fire. The stillness life takes on offers a time of reflection and the perfect excuse for impromptu dinner parties (after all, nothing else is going on).

WINTER PRODUCE

🌿 denotes vegan recipe or easy vegan adaptations given

BLOOD ORANGES

Blood oranges are as delicious as they are gorgeous. The deep crimson flesh has the flavor of an orange crossed with a raspberry. They're usually available for just a month or two before they start to disappear from the markets. With their streaks of red across the orange rind, blood oranges are easy to spot. When buying, choose fruits that are firm but heavy. Juice them while they are in season, and freeze the juice in ice cube trays. Store the blood-red cubes in a large freezer bag for use throughout the year; you'll be glad you did once they become scarce.

BUTTERNUT SQUASH

Butternut squash is easy to fall in love with. The sweet, creamy flesh, with its nutty, candy-like flavors, is perfect in both sweet and savory dishes. Depending on which part of the world you live in, butternut squash may also be known as a butternut pumpkin or a gramma squash. We can all call it delicious and get to cooking, right? Choose a squash without blemishes or soft spots, and favor one with the stem still intact.

GRAPEFRUIT

There is a wide range of colors in the world of grapefruits, from white to red. While most grapefruits tend to be on the sour side, there are a few varieties that lean toward the sweet. For less pucker, seek out the white-fleshed Duncan. For these recipes, I used a sweet-tart pink grapefruit, but feel free to experiment to find what you like. Gently squeeze the fruit all over to make sure it has a uniform give to it; you want to avoid any grapefruit with soft spots.

LEEKS

With the flavor of an onion plus a bit of sweetness, leeks are approachable and versatile. When selecting leeks, look for bunches that are less dark green and more white or light green with firm, crisp leaves. When cooking these recipes, remove and discard the dark green part, using only the pale green and white parts. Make sure to clean them well, as these little beasts are pros at trapping dirt between their layers (see Note on page 202).

LEMONS

Lemons are like a promise. In the deep of winter, we're gifted bright, sunny, beautiful fruit to remind us that the end of the darkness is near. While lemons are fairly easy to source all year long, the peak season for these beauties is late winter. Depending on the area you live in and the variety of lemon you select, the level of sweetness can vary wildly. For these recipes I used the Eureka, a very popular and widely available lemon in the United States. If you opt instead for the sweeter Meyer variety, make sure to adjust the sugar in the recipe down to accommodate the lemon's natural sugars.

ONIONS

Onions are a staple in great cooking, adding everything from texture to flavor to all manner of dishes. From the bite of a raw red onion to the sweetness of a caramelized Vidalia, an onion is not just an onion. When selecting one for a recipe, heed the type that is called for, as they aren't interchangeable. Natural sugar levels, ring thickness, and the ability to hold up or break down during cooking are all qualities that vary from type to type. To take the bite out of a raw onion while still preserving its snap and flavor, dice it and soak it in a bowl of ice water for ten minutes. Drain and then you're ready to go. Always store onions in a cool, dry place, but avoid storing them in a *cold* place (e.g., your fridge). The cold has a tendency to break down the onions. And opt for a paper bag instead of a plastic bag to discourage sprouting.

POTATOES

From the giddy pleasure of French fries to the comfort of a big bowl of mashed potatoes, these root vegetables are always a delight. When choosing a variety to cook with, make sure to pay attention to the texture. Waxy potatoes (golden or red skinned) are better when you intend to keep them in chunks, as the flesh holds up well and caramelizes easily. When looking to mash or fry potatoes, seek out an Idaho or russet, as the high starch content makes them nice and fluffy. Store them in a cool, dark, well-ventilated place, such as a large paper bag with a few holes punched in it in your pantry. Although potatoes are hardy enough to grow in almost any condition year-round, they peak in popularity in the winter, whether because of the lack of other options or the beauty of mashed potatoes at holiday meals. No matter why we consume them in such abundance in the winter; they make an excellent comfort food.

RUTABAGAS

Also known as swedes or neeps, rutabagas are a cross between a turnip and a cabbage. If you can find them with the greens still intact, grab them; they're edible! Add the greens to salads, sauté them, or make pesto with them—all great ways to get a little something extra from your produce haul. Look for rutabagas that are large, bulbous, and very firm. Don't wash them prior to storage, as the added moisture promotes mold. Just toss them in a paper bag and fridge them until ready to use.

Doppelbock Rutabaga Mash with Lemon Confit Butter
page 221

Spiced Rutabaga and Porter Cake with Salted Maple Icing
page 224

SWEET POTATOES

There isn't a vegetable that's more like candy than the sweet potato. True to its name, this root vegetable is sweet and satisfying. Don't be fooled by typical grocery store labeling; a sweet potato is often mistakenly called a yam. A sweet potato has tapered ends and thin, smooth skin, with flesh that can range from light brown to dark orange. A yam is cylindrical and typically white-fleshed, and has rough, dark, almost hairy skin. It's no wonder a yam wants to be a sweet potato! Store them in a paper bag in your pantry, not your fridge. The too-cold temperature of your fridge can actually alter the cell structure of this tuber and diminish its flavor.

Sweet Potato and Winter Ale Soup with Crispy Sage and Pomegranate
page 225

Crispy Sweet Potato Tacos 🌿
page 227

TURNIPS

It's OK if you've mistaken a rutabaga for a turnip or vice versa, as they're close cousins. Turnips are closer to radishes, with a bit of a peppery bite. At the store, look for smaller ones. These are younger, sweeter, and more tender than their bigger counterparts, which tend to be woody and dense. These guys are low maintenance when it comes to storage. Just toss them in your crisper and they can sit there for weeks, even months in some cases. Just make sure you keep them moisture-free and store them without their greens attached.

Roasted Turnips with Whipped Winter Ale Goat Cheese
page 228

Turnip and Belgian Quad Breakfast Hash
page 230

WINTER BEERS

In colder months the produce turns more monochromatic and the offerings are fewer, but the seasonal beer selection more than makes up for that. Of all the seasons, winter offers the most exciting beer options. From the release of long-awaited barrel-aged beers to the growing numbers of winter beer festivals, this is a season to truly celebrate beer. The beers tend to be dark, high ABV, rich, and full of malt. These are sipping beers, sharing beers, beers to be savored and contemplated.

 STOUT AND PORTER. These dark, roasty beers are staples of not only the winter beer-drinking scene, but also the winter cooking-with-beer scene. They're versatile and forgiving, and they lend not only the leavening power of beer to baked goods, but also the flavors of roasted malt. Porters tend to be lighter in color and body, with a touch more bitterness, but when it comes to cooking, the two styles are interchangeable. Look for notes of chocolate, coffee, dark fruit, and bread.

 BARREL-AGED BEER. Winter is punctuated with epic beer release days. Craft beer aficionados will jump a flight and wait in line for hours for the chance to brag about consuming these sought-after beers. Often, these are beers that have been aging in barrels for several seasons and up to several years. Remember, beer is usually aged in barrels that previously held spirits or wine, so they often contain the flavors of the barrel's last resident. They also tend to have high ABVs. These are sipping beers that are not meant to be consumed in great measure all at once.

 WINTER WARMER/HOLIDAY ALE. Although the idea of a "winter ale" varies wildly from brewery to brewery, there are some common themes. Most often, beer that has been designated a winter ale falls into the category of a strong ale (a.k.a. old ale). However, they can also include anything from an IPA to a stout. Winter warmers are generally higher in ABV, have strong malt profiles, range from dark amber to inky black, and frequently contain spices such as cinnamon, nutmeg, or cloves. Their carbonation levels tend to be lower, too.

 BARLEYWINE. Don't let the name fool you, barleywine is very much a beer. It was originally brewed to be an alternative to wine; most of these beers hover near a double-digit ABV, much higher than your standard taproom offerings. Barleywine offers a big malt sweetness and is the perfect choice for cellar aging, often growing in complexity as the years go by.

 BELGIAN QUADRUPEL. Be careful with this beer. The mellow hop profile and pleasantly sweet malt character help these beers go down softly, but they nearly always carry a big stick. Quads most often have an ABV over 10 percent, and it's not uncommon to see one that boasts an ABV over 13 percent. Amber to reddish in color, they often offer flavors of fruit and spice and pair remarkably well with a winter feast.

 DOPPELBOCK. Think of the doppelbock as a bock's big brother or feisty cousin. It's richer, stronger, and bigger on flavor than its mellow little brother. Of all the lagers in the land, this one is the most flavor-forward and food-friendly. Look for notes of caramel, dark fruits, toasted grains, toffee, or raisins.

DRUNKEN WINTER FARRO AND BLOOD ORANGE SALAD
WITH STOUT-BALSAMIC GLAZE

SERVES 4

Blood oranges are so lovely for such a violent name. Their gorgeous flesh does look a little like, well, flesh. But don't let that stop you! They're delicious and magical. Just overlook the fact that your kitchen will look like a citrus slaughterhouse for a moment.

SALAD

1½ cups	winter ale	340 g
1 cup	water	226 g
1 cup	pearled farro	200 g
pinch	kosher salt	

GLAZE

1 cup	balsamic vinegar	240 g
½ cup	stout	113 g
3 tablespoons	honey	42 g

ASSEMBLY

4 cups	baby arugula	120 g
2	blood oranges, peeled and cut between membranes into segments	
½ cup	crumbled goat cheese	75 g
½ cup	candied pecans	68 g

TO MAKE THE FARRO: Combine the beer and water in a small saucepan and bring to a boil over high heat. Stir in the farro and salt and reduce the heat to medium-low. Cover and simmer for 30 minutes or until the farro is cooked but still chewy. Drain the farro and allow it to cool.

TO MAKE THE GLAZE: In a small saucepan, combine the balsamic, stout, and honey. Simmer over medium heat, stirring occasionally, until it has reduced to a syrup, about 15 minutes. Remove the pan from the heat and set it aside.

TO ASSEMBLE: In a large bowl, toss together the arugula, blood orange segments, cooled farro, goat cheese, and pecans. Just before serving, drizzle the glaze over the salad.

BLOODY HELL
(SPICY BLOOD ORANGE BEER COCKTAIL)

I was asked to speak at a conference in New York a few years ago. They asked for a cocktail recipe to serve before my talk, and I offered up this one a few weeks in advance. The conference organizers told me later—after the cocktail was a smashing success—that they were so skeptical of the ingredients that they made it ahead of time to make sure it was good. It was so good, in fact, that they knocked off early to make a second batch.

	freshly squeezed blood	
2 ounces	**orange juice**	57 g
1.5 ounces	**bourbon**	43 g
1 tablespoon	**agave**	18 g
1	**jalapeño, sliced**	
2 ounces	**winter warmer IPA**	57 g

In a shaker filled with ice, combine the blood orange juice, bourbon, agave, and jalapeño. Shake well. Pour the cocktail through a strainer into a highball glass filled with ice. Add the beer, stir, and serve.

NOTE

For a less spicy cocktail, remove the seeds and membrane from the jalapeños—that's where the heat is!

BUTTERNUT SQUASH AND ROASTED GARLIC–GRUYÈRE GRATIN

SERVES 4

Why should potatoes have all the fun? You can gratin anything! Butternut squash, with its inherent sweetness and lovely, nutty flavor, makes the perfect subject to roast all covered in cheese.

1	head garlic	
1 tablespoon	extra virgin olive oil	15 g
1	medium butternut squash, peeled, seeded, and cut into 1-inch-thick half-moons	
3 tablespoons	unsalted butter	42 g
½	large white onion, sliced	
4	large fresh sage leaves, minced	
1 teaspoon, divided	kosher salt	6 g
1 tablespoon	cornstarch	9 g
½ cup	reduced-sodium vegetable broth	114 g
⅓ cup	winter ale	74 g
1 cup	shredded Gruyère	142 g
½ teaspoon	freshly ground black pepper	2 g

Preheat the oven to 425°F.

Remove most of the outer papery skin from the head of garlic. Slice off the top ½ inch or so to expose the tips of all the cloves while keeping the head intact. Place the head on a square of aluminum foil. Drizzle with the olive oil and close the foil tightly around the garlic.

Place the wrapped garlic in a small baking dish and roast until softened, about 40 minutes. Remove the garlic from the oven and set it aside, still wrapped, to cool. Reduce the oven temperature to 400°F.

Meanwhile, lay the butternut squash slices in a 9 × 13-inch baking dish in two tight layers, one on top of the other.

Melt the butter in a saucepan over medium heat. Add the onion slices and cook, stirring occasionally, until they start to caramelize, about 20 minutes. Stir in the sage and ½ teaspoon (3 g) of the salt.

Once the garlic has cooled enough to handle, unwrap and squeeze the head over the saucepan so that the soft cloves drop in. Discard the rest of the head.

Add the cornstarch and stir to combine. Stir in the broth and beer. Add half of the Gruyère, about 2 tablespoons at a time, stirring until combined before adding more.

Pour the mixture over the squash, then top with the remaining Gruyère. Season with the remaining ½ teaspoon (3 g) of salt and the pepper.

Cover the baking dish with aluminum foil and bake the squash for 30 minutes or until a fork easily pierces its flesh. Serve warm.

ROASTED BUTTERNUT SQUASH AND BARREL-AGED STOUT CARAMELIZED ONION PIZZA

SERVES 4

I didn't grow up in a butternut squash household; I discovered its magnificence when I was an adult. Really, it's the pumpkin's fault—it was my gateway squash. And everyone knows that once you experiment with one cool-weather squash, it's only a matter of time before you want more. Kale is used in this recipe because it's an excellent vegetable to seek out toward the end of winter. Although it peaks in the beginning of spring, when the weather is still on the chilly side but the sun has come out to play, kale season actually begins in winter. The overlapping of the vegetable harvests makes for the most amazing flavor combinations. The onions can be made several days in advance. Store them in an airtight container in the fridge until ready to use.

ONIONS

4 tablespoons	unsalted butter	56 g
3	large sweet white onions, thinly sliced	
½ teaspoon	kosher salt	3 g
1 tablespoon, packed	golden brown sugar	14 g
½ cup	barrel-aged stout	113 g

DOUGH

2½ cups	bread flour	317 g
1 (2¼-teaspoon) packet	fast-rising instant yeast	
1 teaspoon	granulated sugar	5 g
½ teaspoon	garlic powder	1.5 g
¾ cup	winter ale	170 g
½ teaspoon	kosher salt	3 g
¼ cup	extra virgin olive oil	60 g

ASSEMBLY

½	large butternut squash, peeled, seeded, and diced	
3 tablespoons	extra virgin olive oil	45 g
for dusting	semolina flour or cornmeal	
½ cup	shredded gouda	57 g
2 cups	chopped lacinato kale	85 g

TO MAKE THE ONIONS: Melt the butter in a large saucepan over medium heat. Add the onions, salt, and sugar and cook, stirring occasionally, until the onions start to soften, about 15 minutes. Add the beer and simmer, stirring occasionally, until the beer is mostly gone. This will take at least 45 minutes but could take up to 2 hours. Keep the heat low to medium to prevent the onions from burning. Set the pan aside.

TO MAKE THE DOUGH: In the bowl of a stand mixer fitted with the dough hook attachment, mix the flour, yeast, sugar, and garlic powder on medium speed until combined.

Put the beer in a microwave-safe bowl. Microwave on high for 20 seconds. Test the beer's temperature with an instant-read thermometer and repeat this process until it registers between 120°F and 125°F or reaches the temperature specified on the package of yeast.

Add the beer to the flour mixture and mix on medium speed until most of the flour has been moistened. With the mixer running, slowly add the salt and oil. Increase the speed to high and beat the dough until it is smooth and elastic, about 8 minutes.

RECIPE CONTINUES ☞

ROASTED BUTTERNUT SQUASH AND BARREL-AGED STOUT CARAMELIZED ONION PIZZA

CONTINUED

Lightly grease a large bowl. Transfer the dough to the bowl and cover it tightly with plastic wrap. Allow the dough to sit in a warm place until it has doubled in size, 45 to 60 minutes.

TO ASSEMBLE: Place a pizza stone in the oven. Preheat the oven to 450°F.

Spread out the butternut squash on a rimmed baking sheet and drizzle with the olive oil. Roast until a fork easily pierces the squash, about 15 minutes. Remove the pan from the oven and raise the oven temperature to 500°F.

Dust a pizza peel with semolina flour or cornmeal. Lightly flour a clean, dry work surface. Turn out the dough and roll it into a 10-inch circle. Transfer it to the prepared pizza peel. Top the dough with the caramelized onions in an even layer. Scatter the cheese and roasted squash on top.

Carefully transfer the pizza to the pizza stone. Bake until golden brown, about 12 minutes.

Remove the pizza from the oven. Top with the kale, slice, and serve.

GRAPEFRUIT–QUAD PIE
WITH BEER MASCARPONE

SERVES 8

It's fun when someone tells you they don't like grapefruit. It's the perfect challenge. Sure, maybe they don't like it raw, but that's no reason to dismiss the beautiful things that happen when it's cooked. This pie, vibrant with winter citrus, is exhibit A when trying to convert people to the grapefruit side. As a bonus, it can be made a day ahead!

DOUGH

1½ cups + more for dusting	all-purpose flour	180+ g
1 teaspoon	kosher salt	6 g
2 tablespoons	granulated sugar	26 g
1 stick	unsalted butter, softened	114 g
3 tablespoons	unsalted butter, chilled and cut into small cubes	42 g
¼ cup	Belgian quadrupel	57 g

FILLING

1¼ cups, divided	freshly squeezed grapefruit juice	295 g
3	large egg yolks	
½ teaspoon	kosher salt	3 g
¼ cup	Belgian quadrupel	57 g
¾ cup	granulated sugar	150 g
3 tablespoons	unsalted butter	42 g
2 tablespoons	cornstarch	18 g

TO MAKE THE DOUGH: Combine the flour, salt, sugar, and softened butter in the bowl of a food processor and process until smooth. Add the cold butter and pulse until just combined. You should still be able to see some larger pieces of butter; this will create flaky layers. Pulse in the beer until it is completely incorporated. The dough will be very soft.

Lay a long sheet of plastic wrap on a work surface. Turn out the dough onto the plastic wrap and form it into a disk about 6 inches in diameter. Wrap the disk tightly in the plastic and refrigerate until firm, about 3 hours or up to 3 days.

Preheat the oven to 350°F.

Lightly flour a clean, dry work surface. Turn out the dough and roll it into a 12-inch circle. Line a 9-inch pie pan with the dough. Prick the bottom of the pie several times with a fork to release air bubbles during baking, then add pie weights or dried beans if desired. (Pie weights will help the pie crust keep its shape.)

Bake until the crust is lightly golden brown, 15 to 18 minutes. Set the crust aside to cool.

TO MAKE THE FILLING: In a bowl, whisk together ½ cup (118 g) of the grapefruit juice, the egg yolks, and the salt.

In a small saucepan, combine the remaining ¾ cup (177 g) of grapefruit juice, the beer, the sugar, the butter, and the cornstarch. Cook over medium heat, stirring frequently, until the butter has melted and the mixture is starting to thicken.

While whisking continuously, slowly pour the hot beer-grapefruit mixture into the bowl with the egg yolk mixture. Whisk until well combined.

Return everything to the saucepan and cook over medium heat, stirring continuously, until the mixture thickens, about 10 minutes.

Transfer the filling to the cooled pie shell and allow the pie to cool to room temperature. Refrigerate until set, about 3 hours, then slice and serve.

GRAPEFRUIT-QUAD PIE

—

PAGE 197

ROSEMARY GRAPEFRUIT SCONES

Sure, scones sound like a breakfast food, but that's not all they are. They're also the perfect afternoon snack or a great way to make your coworkers happy. Unless your office won't let you bring them beer, in which case you may want to consider a career change. Or just sneak in the flavor with these scones and save the beer for happy hour.

2 cups + more for dusting	**all-purpose flour**	240+ g
¼ cup + 1 tablespoon, divided	**granulated sugar**	63 g
2 teaspoons	**baking powder**	8 g
1 teaspoon	**kosher salt**	6 g
1 tablespoon	**grated grapefruit zest**	6 g
1 teaspoon + more for topping	**chopped fresh rosemary leaves**	1.5+ g
5 tablespoons	**unsalted butter, chilled and cut into ½-inch pieces**	70 g
¼ cup	**sour cream**	60 g
¼ cup	**winter ale**	57 g
¼ cup + 1 tablespoon, divided	**freshly squeezed grapefruit juice**	59 g

Preheat the oven to 425°F.

Combine the flour, ¼ cup (50 g) of the sugar, the baking powder, the salt, the zest, and the rosemary in the bowl of a food processor and pulse to combine.

With the food processor running, add the butter cubes, one at a time, through the feed tube and process until well combined. Add the sour cream, beer, and ¼ cup (68 g) of the grapefruit juice and pulse until the dough is just combined. The dough will be soft.

Lightly flour a clean, dry work surface. Turn out the dough and gently pat it into a disk about 1 inch thick. Cut the dough into 8 equal wedges.

Transfer the wedges to a rimmed baking sheet. Brush the tops of the scones with the remaining 1 tablespoon (13 g) grapefruit juice. Sprinkle the remaining 1 tablespoon (13 g) sugar and some rosemary on top.

Bake for 12 minutes or until the edges of the scones are just starting to turn golden brown. Serve warm.

STOUT AND CARAMELIZED LEEK DIP

SERVES 4

When I was a kid, onion dip came out of a packet. It was usually served with generic potato chips and enjoyed near a man-made body of water. I do things a little different these days. The onions in my dip are now leeks. With their sweet, mild flavor, they lend themselves to addictive snacking. It's also a dip that takes a second to come to its full powers. It's great right after being made, but even better the next day. Don't be afraid to make this in advance!

4 tablespoons	**unsalted butter**	56 g
2	**large leeks (see Note), white and pale green parts only, thinly sliced**	
1 tablespoon, packed	**golden brown sugar**	14 g
1 teaspoon, divided	**kosher salt**	6 g
¼ cup	**stout**	57 g
1 pound	**cream cheese, softened**	454 g
1 cup	**sour cream**	240 g
¾ cup	**shredded smoked gouda**	85 g
1 teaspoon	**garlic powder**	3 g
1 teaspoon	**freshly ground black pepper**	2 g
for serving	**potato chips or baguette slices**	

Melt the butter in a large saucepan over medium heat. Add the leeks and sprinkle the brown sugar on top. Cook, stirring occasionally, until the leeks start to soften, about 10 minutes. Stir in ½ teaspoon (3 g) of the salt and the beer. Continue to cook until the leeks have caramelized, about 20 minutes.

Combine the cream cheese, sour cream, gouda, garlic powder, pepper, and remaining ½ teaspoon (3 g) of salt in the bowl of a food processor. Process until smooth. Add the leeks and pulse to combine.

Serve at room temperature with chips or bread, or store in an airtight container in the refrigerator for up to 3 days.

NOTE

To properly wash a leek (these things can trap an impressive amount of dirt!), cut off the root and slice the leek lengthwise to expose the inner layers, where dirt hides. Wash well under cool running water, making sure to remove the grit between the leaves. From there you are ready to slice. If you see any remaining dirt once the leeks have been sliced, put them all in a strainer and rinse again.

BEER-BRAISED LEEKS
WITH LEMON AND PARMIGIANO-REGGIANO VINAIGRETTE

If I challenged you to eat an entire plate of onions, you'd probably call me crazy. But then I'd set down this plate of onion-adjacent vegetables with cheese and butter, and you'd eat the entire thing. It's shocking, really, how lovely and sweet the leek can be with just a little help.

3 tablespoons	unsalted butter	42 g
6	large leeks (see Note on page 202), white and pale green parts only, cut into 1-inch sections	
1 teaspoon	kosher salt	6 g
3	large cloves garlic, minced	
½ cup	stout	113 g
1 teaspoon	grated lemon zest	2 g
¼ cup	freshly squeezed lemon juice	60 g
1 tablespoon	Dijon mustard	15 g
2 tablespoons	white wine vinegar	30 g
¼ cup	freshly grated Parmigiano-Reggiano	25 g
¼ cup	extra virgin olive oil	60 g
¼ cup	chopped pecans	34 g

Melt the butter in a large skillet over medium-high heat. Add the leeks and cook, stirring occasionally, until they start to brown, about 5 minutes. Season with the salt.

Stir in the garlic, then the beer. Reduce the heat to medium and cook, stirring occasionally, for about 10 minutes, until the pan is mostly dry.

Combine the lemon zest, lemon juice, mustard, vinegar, and Parmigiano-Reggiano in the bowl of a food processor and process until well blended. With the machine running, slowly add the oil through the feed tube, blending until well combined.

Transfer the leeks to a serving plate. Drizzle the dressing over the top as desired. Garnish with the pecans and serve immediately.

LEMON-BEER PARTY CAKE
WITH LIME MASCARPONE FROSTING

Party cakes are just what you want them to be. They're much less stress and hassle than a tiered cake, they portion out for a large group, and they're crowd-pleasers. Feel free to add some fresh fruit, candied lemon peel, or brandied cherries—it's a party, after all. This cake can be made a day in advance.

CAKE

2 cups	granulated sugar	400 g
2 tablespoons	grated lemon zest	12 g
2 sticks	unsalted butter	228 g
4	large eggs	
¾ cup	winter ale	170 g
½ cup	whole milk	120 g
3 tablespoons	freshly squeezed lemon juice	66 g
1 teaspoon	pure vanilla extract	5 g
3 cups + more for dusting	all-purpose flour	360+ g
1 teaspoon	baking powder	6 g
1 teaspoon	kosher salt	6 g

FROSTING

1 stick	unsalted butter, softened	114 g
8 ounces	mascarpone	227 g
2 cups	powdered sugar	240 g
2 teaspoons	grated lime zest	4 g

TO MAKE THE CAKE: Preheat the oven to 325°F. Grease and flour a 9 × 13-inch baking dish.

Combine the sugar and lemon zest in the bowl of a stand mixer fitted with the paddle attachment. Mix on high speed for about 2 minutes to help the zest release its oils. Add the butter and beat on high until it is light, fluffy, and well combined with the sugar. Add the eggs, one at a time, beating well after each addition.

Stop the mixer and add the beer, milk, lemon juice, and vanilla. Mix on medium speed to combine. Add the flour, baking power, and salt and mix on low speed until the batter is just combined.

Pour the batter into the prepared baking dish and smooth the top. Bake for 35 to 40 minutes, until the top of the cake springs back when lightly touched. Remove the cake from the oven and allow to cool to room temperature.

TO MAKE THE FROSTING: In the bowl of a stand mixer fitted with the paddle attachment, beat the butter and mascarpone on medium speed until well combined. Add the powdered sugar and lime zest and mix until well combined.

Spread the frosting over the cake. Refrigerate for at least 1 hour or until ready to serve.

FETTUCCINE
WITH ROASTED CHICKPEAS AND KALE IN
LEMON AND BELGIAN ALE CREAM SAUCE

SERVES 4

For a cold-weather meal, this tastes as bright as sunshine. One taste of the freshness of the kale and the pop of the lemon and you'll be transported. We also need to take a second to mention the delightful crunch of the chickpeas, so addictive and crispy you might need to make a batch just for snacking.

1 (15.5-ounce) can	chickpeas, rinsed and drained	369 g
2 tablespoons	extra virgin olive oil	30 g
½ teaspoon + more to taste	kosher salt	3+ g
½ teaspoon + more to taste	freshly ground black pepper	2+ g
½ teaspoon	chili powder	1.5 g
1 pound	fettuccine	
5 tablespoons	unsalted butter	70 g
3	cloves garlic, minced	
1 cup	Belgian quadrupel	227 g
½ cup	half-and-half	112 g
2 tablespoons	freshly squeezed lemon juice	30 g
½ cup	shredded Parmigiano-Reggiano	50 g
2 cups	chopped kale	85 g

Preheat the oven to 425°F.

Dry the chickpeas between paper towels or clean dishtowels until they are completely dry to the touch. Spread out the chickpeas in a single layer on a rimmed baking sheet. Add the olive oil and salt, tossing to coat the chickpeas.

Roast until the chickpeas are golden brown and crispy, about 20 minutes. Transfer the roasted chickpeas to a bowl. Add the black pepper and chili powder, tossing to coat.

Cook the pasta according to the package directions until just before it is al dente. Drain and set aside.

Melt the butter in a sauté pan over medium-high heat. Add the garlic and cook until fragrant, about 30 seconds. Add the beer, half-and-half, and lemon juice and reduce the heat to medium to maintain a simmer. Add the Parmigiano-Reggiano, about 1 tablespoon at a time, stirring until melted before adding more. Simmer the sauce until it thickens. Stir in the kale. Season with salt and pepper to taste.

Combine the pasta and sauce in a serving dish. Add the chickpeas and toss before serving.

BARLEYWINE-PICKLED ONIONS

Pickle your own onions once and you'll be hooked. You'll find yourself adding them to tacos, salads, and sandwiches—or just eating them right out of the jar. It's a fantastically simple way to add a little pop of brightness and a hint of the flavors of a perfectly malty beer to just about any meal.

1½ cups	barleywine	340 g
1 cup	apple cider vinegar	240 g
2 tablespoons	kosher salt	36 g
1 tablespoon	granulated sugar	13 g
1 tablespoon	whole black peppercorns	8 g
1	medium red onion, thinly sliced	

Combine the beer, vinegar, salt, sugar, and peppercorns in a small saucepan. Bring to a simmer over medium-high heat and cook, stirring constantly, until the sugar and salt dissolve. Remove the pan from the heat.

Put the onion slices in an airtight container. Pour the brine over the onion. Allow to sit at room temperature until cooled. Cover and refrigerate the pickled onion for at least 1 day or up to 1 week.

MUSHROOM AND GOUDA STUFFED BARLEYWINE ONIONS

Don't be afraid of stuffed onions—they only sound like they will ruin your breath. Once you add a long visit to a hot oven, the bitter bite of a raw onion is replaced with a mellow sweetness that complements the Thanksgiving dressing–style filling. The heartiness elevates these onions to entrée-worthy status, making this an excellent dish to serve during the holidays for anyone who prefers vegetables.

6	medium white onions	
2 tablespoons	extra virgin olive oil	30 g
3–5 cups	barleywine	780–1,180 g
3 tablespoons, divided	unsalted butter	42 g
1	large leek (see Note on page 202), white and pale green parts only, thinly sliced	
1 pound	chanterelles, chopped	454 g
½ cup	bread crumbs	65 g
1 teaspoon	chopped fresh sage leaves	0.5 g
1 teaspoon	chopped fresh rosemary leaves	0.5 g
¼ cup	half-and-half	60 g
2 cups	shredded gouda	120 g

Preheat the oven to 350°F. Line a rimmed baking sheet with aluminum foil.

Peel off the papery outer skin from the onions. Slice off the top one-third from the pointier end of each. Slice off the root just enough to make the onion sit flat, cut side up. Using a melon baller, hollow out each onion, leaving about ½ inch of the walls intact. (Reserve the onion innards for another use.)

Stand the hollowed onions in a baking dish and brush their insides with the olive oil. Pour enough beer into the dish to reach about halfway up the sides of the onions. Roast until softened, about 40 minutes.

Melt 1 tablespoon (14 g) of the butter in a sauté pan over medium heat. Add the leek and cook, stirring occasionally, until softened and starting to caramelize, about 10 minutes.

Add the remaining 2 tablespoons (28 g) of butter, stirring until melted. Stir in the chanterelles. Cook, stirring occasionally, until the chanterelles are darkened and softened, about 15 minutes. Sprinkle with the bread crumbs, sage, and rosemary and stir until the chanterelles are well coated. Pour in the half-and-half and stir until the mixture is well combined and thickened, about 3 minutes.

Transfer the roasted onions to the prepared baking sheet. Fill them with the chanterelle mixture. Top each stuffed onion with some of the gouda.

Bake until the cheese has melted, about 10 minutes. Serve warm.

THE
SHEPHERD'S
GARDEN PIE

PAGE 216

THE SHEPHERD'S GARDEN PIE

SERVES 4 TO 6

When I was in fourth grade, the teachers had us interview each other for a class project. One of the questions was "What's your favorite food?" I wasn't the sort to follow the crowd. While everyone else said "pizza," I said "shepherd's pie" and just waited for their judgment. But, as fate would have it, nearly every kid had a mom who'd made it with Thanksgiving leftovers, and they gave me a pass. It also turns out that shepherd's pie is not as dependent on meat as one may think. It's all about the gravy and mashed potatoes, which go well with just about any vegetable you can pull out of your garden.

TOPPING

3	large russet potatoes, peeled and quartered	
1 stick	unsalted butter	114 g
¾ cup	sour cream	180 g
1 teaspoon	kosher salt	6 g
1 teaspoon	garlic powder	3 g

FILLING

4 tablespoons	unsalted butter	56 g
2	large carrots, peeled and diced	
1	rib celery, diced	
1	medium white onion, chopped	
1	large leek (see Note on page 202), white and pale green parts only, sliced	
8 ounces	cremini mushrooms, sliced	227 g
1	small butternut squash, peeled, seeded, and diced	
1 cup, divided	stout	227 g
2 tablespoons	all-purpose flour	16 g
1 teaspoon	kosher salt	6 g
1 teaspoon	freshly ground black pepper	4 g
1 teaspoon	chopped fresh rosemary leaves	1.5 g
1 cup	reduced-sodium vegetable broth	240 g
¼ cup	heavy cream	60 g

TO MAKE THE TOPPING: Bring a large pot of salted water to a boil over high heat. Add the potatoes and cook until a fork easily pierces them, about 15 minutes.

Drain the potatoes and transfer to large bowl. Add the butter, sour cream, salt, and garlic powder. With a hand mixer set on medium speed, beat the potatoes until they are light and fluffy.

TO MAKE THE FILLING: Preheat the oven to 375°F.

Melt the butter in a large skillet over medium-high heat. Add the carrots, celery, onion, and leek and cook, stirring occasionally, until the vegetables start to brown, about 5 minutes.

Stir in the mushrooms and cook until they darken and soften, about 10 minutes. Stir in the butternut squash. Add ½ cup (113.5 g) of the beer, reduce the heat to medium, and partially cover the pan. Simmer until most of the beer is gone and the squash is tender, about 15 minutes.

Stir in the flour, salt, pepper, and rosemary. Add the remaining ½ cup (113.5 g) of beer and the broth and simmer until thickened, about 10 minutes. Stir in the cream and remove the pan from the heat.

Pour the filling into a 9 × 13-inch baking dish. Cover it with the mashed potatoes in an even layer. Bake for 15 minutes or until the potatoes start to brown. Serve immediately.

BEER SAMOSAS
WITH WINTER RAITA DIPPING SAUCE

Samosas are the Middle East's answer to the hand pie. Small, portable, and full of mashed potatoes, they are just as satisfying as they sound. It's like fries and a pie mixed together! It's also pretty simple, especially for deep-fried food, and worth the extra effort. Raita, the dipping sauce, has been updated from the traditional cucumber and cilantro–spiked version that's perfect for the warmer months to a similar sauce that uses the herbs of winter.

DOUGH

1½ cups	all-purpose flour	180 g
1 teaspoon	kosher salt	6 g
4 tablespoons	unsalted butter, cubed	56 g
⅓ cup	winter ale	74 g

FILLING AND SERVING

2 tablespoons	extra virgin olive oil	30 g
1	medium white onion, diced	
2	large Yukon gold potatoes, peeled and diced	
½ cup	fresh or frozen peas	75 g
1 teaspoon	kosher salt	6 g
1 teaspoon	garam masala	3 g
1 teaspoon	garlic powder	3 g
½ teaspoon	ground cumin	1.5 g
¼ teaspoon	curry powder	0.75 g
¼ teaspoon	cayenne pepper	0.75 g
¾ cup	winter ale	170 g
for frying	canola, peanut, or safflower oil	

DIPPING SAUCE

1 cup	plain whole-milk yogurt	240 g
2 tablespoons	minced fresh flat-leaf parsley leaves	2 g
1 teaspoon	minced fresh rosemary leaves	1 g
1 teaspoon	minced fresh thyme leaves	1 g
1 tablespoon	freshly squeezed lemon juice	15 g
1 teaspoon	kosher salt	6 g

TO MAKE THE DOUGH: Combine the flour and salt in the bowl of a food processor and pulse to combine. Add the butter and process until combined. With the food processor running, add the beer through the feed tube and process until the dough comes together.

Form the dough into a ball, place it on a plate, and loosely cover it with a clean dish towel. Set aside to rest for 15 minutes.

RECIPE CONTINUES ☞

TO MAKE THE FILLING: Heat the olive oil in a sauté pan over medium-high heat. Add the onion and cook, stirring occasionally, until softened, about 5 minutes. Add the potatoes, peas, salt, garam masala, garlic powder, cumin, curry, and cayenne and stir until well combined. Stir in half of the beer, reduce the heat to medium, cover, and simmer until the beer is mostly gone, about 10 minutes. Stir in the remaining beer, scraping the bottom of the pan to deglaze it. Cook until the beer is mostly gone and the potatoes are fork-tender, about 10 more minutes.

Mash the potatoes with a potato masher until most (but not all) of the potatoes are mashed. Transfer the potato mixture to a medium bowl.

TO ASSEMBLE: Divide the dough into 6 equal portions. One at a time, roll the portions into thin circles about 6 inches in diameter. Cut each circle in half.

Form each half circle into a cone by pressing the cut edge together. Form an "O" with your thumb and forefinger and set the cone, point side down, in the "O." Fill the cone with 1 to 2 tablespoons of the filling. Moisten the open edge of the dough with water and pinch it closed to seal. Repeat this process with the remaining dough and filling.

TO FRY: Heat 2 inches of oil in a deep saucepan over medium-high heat until a deep-fry thermometer reads 350°F. Add the samosas, a few at a time so as not to crowd the pan, and cook on both sides until golden brown, about 3 minutes per side. Transfer them to a paper towel–lined plate to drain and cool slightly.

TO MAKE THE DIPPING SAUCE: Stir together the yogurt, parsley, rosemary, thyme, lemon juice, and salt in a bowl. Taste and adjust the seasoning as needed.

Serve the samosas warm with the dipping sauce.

NOTE

Peas can be found in limited quantities in early winter; in some locations it's the shoulder of their season. If you're savvy with your in-season peas when they're in abundance where you live, they are an excellent candidate for shelling and freezing in batches.

DOPPELBOCK RUTABAGA MASH
WITH LEMON CONFIT BUTTER

SERVES 4

Why don't we mash more things? Potatoes are always in the mashed-things spotlight, but plenty of other things could use a good mashing. Barley is mashed to make beer, and that just makes life worth living. There was the M*A*S*H TV show that my mom would binge-watch in reruns when I was little, and even the Mansion-Apartment-Shack-House game we'd play as kids. Mashed things need to take more priority in our lives, and we should start with rutabagas.

2	large lemons	
4	large cloves garlic, peeled	
1 teaspoon	whole cloves	1 g
	extra virgin olive oil	
1 large	rutabaga, peeled and chopped	907 g
⅓ cup	reduced-sodium vegetable broth	78 g
¼ cup	doppelbock	57 g
¼ cup	sour cream	60 g
1 teaspoon, divided	kosher salt	6 g
1 stick	unsalted butter, softened	114 g
1 teaspoon	chopped fresh thyme leaves	1 g

Using a vegetable peeler, peel long strips of peel from the lemons, getting as little pith (white part underneath) as possible.

Combine the lemon peels, garlic, and cloves in a small saucepan. Pour in enough olive oil so that everything is just covered. Turn the heat to medium-low and bring the oil to a very low simmer (just a few bubbles but not boiling). Simmer for about 20 minutes, until the lemon peels start to brown at the edges. Remove the pan from the heat and allow the lemon peels to steep until the oil has cooled.

Bring a large pot of salted water to a boil over high heat. Add the rutabaga and cook until a fork easily pierces the rutabaga, about 30 minutes. Drain and return the rutabaga to the pot.

Remove the garlic cloves from the oil and add them to the rutabaga, along with the vegetable broth, beer, sour cream, and ½ teaspoon (3 g) of the salt. Using a hand mixer set on medium speed, beat until the rutabaga is fluffy and all the ingredients are well combined.

Remove the peels from the oil (save the oil for another use) and mince the peels. Put them in a small bowl. Add the butter, thyme, and remaining ½ teaspoon (3 g) of salt and mix until well combined.

Serve the rutabaga mash topped with the lemon butter.

SPICED
RUTABAGA
AND PORTER
CAKE
―
PAGE 224

SPICED RUTABAGA AND PORTER CAKE
WITH SALTED MAPLE ICING

SERVES 8

This is a cake that you may want to be a bit elusive about before serving. After all, if you tell your guests that you're serving them a "vegan rutabaga cake," you may not have many takers. On second thought, that might not be a bad idea: it's so moist and delicious that you may want to keep it all to yourself.

CAKE

1	small rutabaga, peeled and chopped	
1¾ cups	all-purpose flour	210 g
¾ cup, packed	golden brown sugar	135 g
1½ teaspoons	baking soda	9 g
1½ teaspoons	baking powder	8 g
½ teaspoon	ground ginger	1.5 g
½ teaspoon	ground cinnamon	1.5 g
½ teaspoon	ground allspice	1.5 g
¼ teaspoon	ground nutmeg	0.75 g
¼ cup	pure maple syrup	78 g
½ cup	vegetable oil	120 g
½ cup	porter	113 g

ICING

2 cups	powdered sugar	240 g
2 teaspoons	kosher salt	12 g
¼ cup	pure maple syrup	60 g
1 tablespoon	water	10 g

TO MAKE THE CAKE: Preheat the oven to 350°F. Grease an 8.5 × 4.5-inch loaf pan.

Bring a large pot of salted water to a boil over high heat. Add the rutabaga and cook until a fork easily pierces the rutabaga, about 30 minutes. Drain the rutabaga, transfer it to a mixing bowl, and mash it with a potato masher. Measure out 1 cup (220 g) of the mashed rutabaga, reserving the rest for another use.

In a mixing bowl, stir together the flour, brown sugar, baking soda, baking powder, ginger, cinnamon, allspice, and nutmeg. Make a well in the dry ingredients. Add the rutabaga mash, maple syrup, oil, and beer to the center of the well and stir until just combined.

Pour the batter into the prepared pan and smooth the top. Bake until the cake is golden brown and a toothpick inserted into the center comes back with just a few moist crumbs, about 40 minutes.

Allow the cake to cool in the pan, then transfer it to a serving plate.

TO MAKE THE ICING: Whisk together the sugar, salt, maple syrup, and water until well combined. Pour the icing over the cake and serve.

SWEET POTATO AND WINTER ALE SOUP
WITH CRISPY SAGE AND POMEGRANATE

SERVES 4

Is there anything more comforting than sweet potato soup? It rides that line between sweet and savory, satisfying a bit of each craving. Making it—and then eating it—is the perfect way to spend a lazy Sunday afternoon in winter.

4 tablespoons	**unsalted butter**	56 g
¼ cup	**chopped shallot**	32 g
3 tablespoons	**all-purpose flour**	27 g
1 tablespoon, packed	**golden brown sugar**	14 g
1½ cups	**winter ale**	340 g
1½ cups	**reduced-sodium vegetable broth**	360 g
2	**large sweet potatoes, peeled and sliced**	
½ teaspoon	**kosher salt**	3 g
½ teaspoon	**freshly ground black pepper**	2 g
¼ teaspoon	**cayenne pepper**	0.5 g
¼ cup	**heavy cream**	60 g
2 tablespoons	**extra virgin olive oil**	30 g
¼ cup	**small fresh sage leaves**	7 g
½ cup	**pomegranate seeds (see Note on page 155)**	122 g

Melt the butter in a large pot or Dutch oven over medium-high heat. Add the shallot and cook, stirring occasionally, until softened. Sprinkle in the flour and cook, stirring constantly, until the mixture is well combined and thickened and the flour has browned, about 5 minutes.

Add the brown sugar, beer, and broth, stirring to combine. Add the sweet potatoes and cook until a fork easily pierces the potatoes, about 20 minutes.

Remove the pot from the heat. Using an immersion blender, blend the mixture until smooth. Stir in the salt, black pepper, cayenne, and heavy cream.

Heat the olive oil in a small saucepan over medium-high heat until hot but not smoking. Add the sage leaves and fry on both sides until crispy, about 10 seconds per side. Transfer the leaves to paper towels to drain.

Portion the soup into bowls. Top each serving with some fried sage leaves and pomegranate seeds and serve.

CRISPY SWEET POTATO TACOS

If anyone ever tells you they could never eat vegan food, your mission is clear. Sit them down, serve them a beer, and feed them as many of these tacos as they can stuff in their face. Because that's what they'll do with these tacos: stuff them in their face by the fistful, unable to argue about anything. Garnet sweet potatoes are often mislabeled in grocery stores as yams. Don't let that deter you, as you know the truth: these dark orange–skinned beauties aren't yams at all; they're most certainly sweet potatoes.

2	large garnet sweet potatoes, cut into ½-inch-thick wedges	
1 tablespoon + 1 teaspoon, divided	kosher salt	24 g
1½ cups	winter ale	340 g
2 tablespoons	extra virgin olive oil	30 g
½ teaspoon	onion powder	1.5 g
½ teaspoon	garlic powder	1.5 g
½ teaspoon	freshly ground black pepper	2 g
12	corn tortillas	
1 cup	frozen corn kernels, thawed	175 g
1	avocado, peeled, pitted, and diced	
½	medium white onion, chopped	38 g
¼ cup	chopped fresh cilantro leaves	6 g
for serving	hot pepper sauce	

Put the sweet potato wedges in a large, shallow bowl. Sprinkle 1 tablespoon (18 g) of the salt over them and add the beer. Add enough water to fully submerge the potato wedges. Cover the bowl and refrigerate for at least 3 hours and up to 12 hours.

Position a rack in the top third of the oven. Place a rimmed baking sheet on the rack. Preheat the oven to 425°F.

Drain the potatoes and rinse well. Pat them dry with paper towels, removing as much moisture as possible to help them crisp. Transfer them to a large bowl. Add the olive oil, onion powder, garlic powder, pepper, and remaining 1 teaspoon (6 g) of salt and toss to coat.

Transfer the potatoes to the preheated baking sheet and spread them out in a single layer. Bake for 15 minutes. Flip the potatoes over and bake for an additional 10 minutes or until the undersides are golden brown. Remove the potatoes from the oven and transfer to paper towels to drain.

Top each tortilla with 2 or 3 sweet potato wedges and some of the corn, avocado, onion, cilantro, and hot sauce. Serve.

ROASTED TURNIPS
WITH WHIPPED WINTER ALE GOAT CHEESE

SERVES 4

You're probably here because you got a turnip in your CSA basket and you have no idea what to do with it. Well, I'm glad you're here. Turnips can actually be quite delightful. Sort of a potato-radish hybrid, these little guys may become something you seek out.

1	small turnip, peeled and cut into 1-inch cubes	
3 tablespoons	unsalted butter, melted	42 g
½ teaspoon	kosher salt	3 g
½ teaspoon	dried oregano	1.5 g
½ teaspoon	garlic powder	1.5 g
1¼ cups	crumbled goat cheese	188 g
¼ cup	winter ale	47 g
½ cup	heavy cream	120 g
2 teaspoons	minced fresh flat-leaf parsley leaves	0.75 g

Preheat the oven to 425°F.

Spread out the turnip in a single layer on a rimmed baking sheet. Drizzle the melted butter on top. Season with the salt, oregano, and garlic powder.

Bake for 15 minutes. Flip the turnip over and bake until a fork easily pierces the cubes, about 10 more minutes.

In a medium bowl, combine the goat cheese and beer and beat until well combined. In a separate bowl, use a hand mixer set on medium speed to beat the cream until medium peaks form. Gently fold the whipped cream and parsley into the goat cheese.

Transfer the turnip to a serving dish. Top with the whipped goat cheese and serve.

TURNIP AND BELGIAN QUAD BREAKFAST HASH

SERVES 2 TO 4

I probably shouldn't have named this "breakfast hash," since you can and should eat it at all hours. And I'm not just talking about mealtimes—it's a pretty great accompaniment to a 3:00 a.m. movie marathon.

2 tablespoons	**extra virgin olive oil**	30 g
½	**large white onion, diced**	
½	**small butternut squash, peeled, seeded, and diced**	
2	**medium red potatoes, diced**	
2	**large turnips, peeled and diced**	
1 teaspoon	**kosher salt**	6 g
¾ cup	**Belgian quadrupel**	170 g
2 cups	**chopped lacinato kale**	85 g
½ teaspoon	**garlic powder**	1.5 g
½ teaspoon	**freshly ground black pepper**	2 g
¼ teaspoon	**sweet paprika**	0.75 g
¼ teaspoon	**ground cumin**	0.75 g
½ teaspoon	**chili powder**	1.5 g
4	**large eggs, poached (see Note on page 41)**	

Heat the olive oil in a large pan over medium-high heat. Add the onion and cook, stirring occasionally, until it starts to brown. Add the butternut squash, potatoes, and turnips. Season with the salt. Cook until the vegetables start to brown, about 10 minutes.

Stir in the beer. Partially cover the pan, reduce the heat to medium, and simmer, stirring occasionally, until the pan is mostly dry and the vegetables have softened, about 10 minutes.

Stir in the kale, garlic powder, pepper, paprika, cumin, and chili powder. Cook until the kale has wilted, about 5 minutes. Serve topped with the poached eggs.

ACKNOWLEDGMENTS

WRITING A BOOK UPSETS THE BALANCE OF YOUR LIFE, what with the late nights, off-kilter schedules, and obsessively staring into the distance when you should be paying attention to a conversation. In response, the people in your life have to shift to accommodate the new mistress taking up your time and invading your thoughts; for that, they should be acknowledged. Without them, books wouldn't exist in their current forms.

First, the people who also had their hands in this book made it what it is today. Jessica Easto for polishing this manuscript in a way I never could have. Ashley Collom for pushing an idea into a concrete concept, and then finding it a home.

My people, who cheered me on as I trudged through the process and brought support and encouragement when it felt never-ending. Nick, my rock, for everything, always. Claire, for being a constant source of inspiration. Cori, for being the person I can always count on, no matter what I need. Alex, for her huge heart and constant entertainment. Addison, for her sweet and feisty spirit. Paulette, for being my consummate cheerleader—you'll never know how much I need that.

When the concept of this book was just starting to stir to life, it was during a difficult period of my life, and several people held me together as I pushed the pieces of this idea into shape. Without their compassion and friendship, this book wouldn't exist: Andi McGrew, Linda Miller, Janell Dastrup, Shelly Ebeling, Allan Murphy, Chris Dodd, Vanessa Bassett, Wendy Samson, Douglas Bailey, and so many more strong and amazing people who have let me into their lives.

RECIPE INDEX BY MEAL TYPE

 denotes vegan recipe or easy vegan adaptations given

APPETIZERS

Beer-Braised Artichokes Wrapped in Puff Pastry | 36

Beer-Steamed Artichokes with Roasted Garlic Hummus | 38

Cucumber Cups with Avocado White Ale Bean Purée | 105

Spicy Beer Pickles | 106

Cilantro, Beer, and Cream Cheese Crostini with Cherry Salsa and ISA-Candied Jalapeños | 110

Flatbreads with Beer-Pickled Peaches, Jalapeño, and Mozzarella | 114

Fried Beer-Battered Tomatillo and Mozzarella Sliders | 119

Black Bean and Farro Stuffed Cabbage Rolls with Brown Ale and Tamarind Sauce | 139

Honey and Ale Roasted Carrot Tart with Carrot Green Pesto | 145

Mexican Street Corn Beer Cakes with Chipotle Crema | 154

Brown Ale Baklava with Baked Brie and Figs | 162

Stout and Caramelized Leek Dip | 202

Beer Samosas with Winter Raita Dipping Sauce | 217

BREAKFAST

Chocolate-Hazelnut Beet Muffins | 51

Beer Polenta with Creamy Chard and Eggs | 77

Blueberry-Lavender Summer Ale Clafoutis | 99

Gochujang and ISA Shakshuka | 124

Ginger Beer Scones | 166

Coconut-Fig French Toast Casserole | 161

Rosemary Grapefruit Scones | 201

Turnip and Belgian Quad Breakfast Hash | 230

SIDE DISHES

Pan-Seared Asparagus with Poached Egg and Beer Béarnaise Sauce | 41

Shaved Asparagus Salad with Lemon-Pilsner Vinaigrette | 42

Salt-Roasted Golden Beets with Whipped Belgian Ale Mascarpone and Herb Gremolata | 49

English Pea and Bock Risotto | 53

Kale Panzanella with Toasted Beer Bread | 58

Grilled Romaine with IPA-Pickled Strawberries | 71

Bing Cherry and Hefeweizen Farro Salad with Mirin-Lime Dressing | 102

Jalapeño-Kölsch Cornbread | 109

Grilled Peaches with ISA-Mint Chimichurri | 116

Watermelon and Feta Salad with Beer-Pickled Onions | 127

Roasted Cabbage Wedges with Feta-Mustard Beer Vinaigrette | 141

Honey and Ale Roasted Carrot Tart with Carrot Green Pesto | 145

Brown Sugar and Oktoberfest Glazed Carrots | 146

Roasted Cauliflower with Creamy Beer and Leek Sauce | 150

Mexican Street Corn Beer Cakes with Chipotle Crema | 154

Black Bean and Grilled Corn Salad with Queso Fresco and Fresh Hop Dressing | 153

Mirin and Ale Caramelized Brussels Sprouts with Goat Cheese and Pomegranate | 155

Drunken Winter Farro and Blood Orange Salad with Stout-Balsamic Glaze | 189

INDEX